W9-AGF-814

the crochet CLOSET

LEISURE ARTS, INC.
Little Rock, Arkansas

EDITORIAL STAFF
Editor-in-Chief: Susan White Sullivan
Knit and Crochet Publications Director: Debra Nettles
Special Projects Director: Susan Frantz Wiles
Senior Prepress Director: Mark Hawkins
Art Publications Director: Rhonda Shelby
Technical Editor: Lois J. Long
Assistant Technical Editors: Cathy Hardy, Linda Daley,
    and Sarah J. Green
Editorial Writer: Susan McManus Johnson
Art Category Manager: Lora Puls
Graphic Artists: Angela Stark and Dayle Carozza
Production Artist: Janie Wright
Imaging Technicians: Brian Hall, Stephanie Johnson,
    and Mark R. Potter
Photography Manager: Katherine Laughlin
Contributing Photographer: Jason Masters
Contributing Photo Stylist: Angela Alexander
Publishing Systems Administrator: Becky Riddle
Publishing Systems Assistants: Clint Hanson
    and John Rose

BUSINESS STAFF
Vice President and Chief Operations Officer:
    Tom Siebenmorgen
Director of Finance and Administration:
    Laticia Mull Dittrich
Vice President, Sales and Marketing: Pam Stebbins
National Accounts Director: Martha Adams
Sales and Services Director: Margaret Reinold
Information Technology Director: Hermine Linz
Controller: Francis Caple
Vice President, Operations: Jim Dittrich
Comptroller, Operations: Rob Thieme
Retail Customer Service Manager: Stan Raynor
Print Production Manager: Fred F. Pruss

Copyright © 2009 by Leisure Arts, Inc., 5701 Ranch Drive, Little
Rock, AR 72223. All rights reserved. This publication is protected
under federal copyright laws. Reproduction of this publication or any
other Leisure Arts publication, including publications which are out
of print, is prohibited unless specifically authorized. This includes,
but is not limited to, any form of reproduction or distribution on
or through the Internet, including posting, scanning or e-mail
transmission. We have made every effort to ensure that these
instructions are accurate and complete. We cannot, however, be
responsible for human error, typographical mistakes or variations in
individual work. Made in the United States of America.

Library of Congress Control Number: 2009935746

ISBN-13: 978-1-60140-135-9
ISBN-10: 1-60140-135-3

Contents

Do you dream of opening your closet each day and finding the perfect outfit ready and waiting? If you crochet, you can make that dream a reality! These feminine fashions by Lisa Gentry give you the key pieces to finish any outfit with unique flair and confidence. For work or play, pair your favorite slacks, skirts, dresses, and jeans with dressy or casual sweaters, vests, and jackets. Fun, figure-enhancing, casual, or elegant—the look that suits your mood is yours with crochet!

"My nieces are my favorite models," says Lisa Gentry. "When I create new designs, they help me by trying them on. It is so much fun to be able to involve my family in my work."

As a designer of crochet and knitting patterns, Lisa is always finding new ways to improve or embellish those arts. Many fans of crochet know Lisa Gentry as the Guinness Book of Records Fastest Crocheter. She's also America's fastest knitter, currently holding that title with the Craft Yarn Council of America.

Lisa grew up in Germany and now lives in Louisiana with her husband. Although she was recently invited to appear on local television to showcase her skills, she regretfully refused, saying, "I'm putting all my time into designing right now."

To join Lisa's online crochet forum and see what she's working on today, visit www.crochetsoiree.com/community. Click on "Groups" and "Leisurely Lisa."

To find more of Lisa Gentry's innovative techniques and patterns, visit your local yarn shop or www.leisurearts.com.

Meet Lisa Gentry

Carefree Cardigan

■■■□ INTERMEDIATE

Size	Finished Chest Measurement
Extra Small	34¹/₂" (87.5 cm)
Small	38¹/₄" (97 cm)
Medium	42" (106.5 cm)
Large	46" (117 cm)
Extra Large	51¹/₂" (131 cm)
2X-Large	55¹/₄" (140.5 cm)
3X-Large	59" (150 cm)

Size Note: Instructions are written for size Extra Small with sizes Small, Medium, and Large in first set of braces { } and sizes Extra Large, 2X-Large, and 3X-Large in second set of braces. Instructions will be easier to read if you circle all the numbers pertaining to your size. If only one number is given, it applies to all sizes.

MATERIALS

Medium Weight Yarn
 [3 ounces, 185 yards
 (85 grams, 170 meters) per skein]:
  6{7-7-8}{8-9-10} skeins
Crochet hooks, sizes H (5 mm) **and** I (5.5 mm)
 or sizes needed for gauge
Sewing needle and thread
1¹/₂" (4 cm) Button

GAUGE: With larger size hook, in pattern,
 (3 dc, ch 1) 4 times = 3³/₄" (9.5 cm)
 8 rows = 4" (10 cm)

Gauge Swatch: 4¹/₂"w x 4"h (11.5 cm x 10 cm)
With larger size hook, ch 21.
Row 1: Dc in fourth ch from hook **(3 skipped chs count as first dc)** and in next ch, work Bobble, ★ skip next ch, work Cluster, work Bobble; repeat from ★ 2 times **more**, skip next ch, dc in last 3 chs.
Row 2: Ch 3 **(counts as first dc, now and throughout)**, turn; dc in next 2 dc, ch 1, skip next Bobble, ★ 3 dc in next Cluster, ch 1, skip next Bobble; repeat from ★ across to last 3 dc, dc in last 3 dc: 15 dc and 4 chs.
Row 3: Ch 3, turn; dc in next 2 dc, work Bobble, skip next ch, ★ work Cluster, work Bobble, skip next ch; repeat from ★ across to last 3 dc, dc in last 3 dc.
Rows 4-8: Repeat Rows 2 and 3 twice, then repeat Row 2 once **more**.
Finish off.

Instructions continued on page 6.

Cardigan

STITCH GUIDE

BOBBLE

Ch 3, YO, insert hook in third ch from hook, YO and pull up a loop, YO and draw through 2 loops on hook, YO, insert hook in same ch, YO and pull up a loop, YO and draw through 2 loops on hook, YO and draw through all 3 loops on hook.

CLUSTER (uses 3 sts)

★ YO, insert hook in **next** st, YO and pull up a loop, YO and draw through 2 loops on hook; repeat from ★ 2 times **more**, YO and draw through all 4 loops on hook.

DOUBLE CROCHET DECREASE

(abbreviated dc decrease) (uses next 2 dc)

★ YO, insert hook in **next** dc, YO and pull up a loop, YO and draw through 2 loops on hook; repeat from ★ once **more**, YO and draw through all 3 loops on hook (counts as one dc).

YOKE

With smaller size hook,
ch 130{132-136-136}{141-141-146}.

Row 1: Sc in second ch from hook and in each ch across: 129{131-135-135}{140-140-145} sc.

Yoke is worked in Back Loops Only through Row 17 *(Fig. 1, page 125)*.

Row 2 (Right side): Ch 1, turn; sc in each sc across.

Note: Loop a short piece of yarn around any stitch to mark Row 2 as **right** side.

Row 3: Ch 1, turn; sc in each sc across increasing 7{10-12-12}{12-15-18} sc evenly spaced *(see Increasing Evenly Across a Row, page 126)*: 136{141-147-147}{152-155-163} sc.

Row 4: Ch 1, turn; sc in each sc across.

Row 5: Ch 1, turn; sc in each sc across increasing 11{14-16-16}{19-24-28} sc evenly spaced: 147{155-163-163}{171-179-191} sc.

Rows 6 and 7: Ch 1, turn; sc in each sc across.

Row 8 (Increase row): Ch 1, turn; sc in each sc across increasing 18{20-22-28}{30-32-33} sc evenly spaced: 165{175-185-191}{201-211-224} sc.

Rows 9-15: Repeat Rows 7 and 8, 3 times; then repeat Row 7 once **more**: 219{235-251-275}{291-307-323} sts.

Begin working in both loops.

Row 16: Ch 3 (counts as first dc, now and throughout), turn; dc in next 2 sc, work Bobble, ★ skip next sc, work Cluster, work Bobble; repeat from ★ across to last 4 sc, skip next sc, dc in last 3 sc: 53{57-61-67}{71-75-79} Clusters, 54{58-62-68}{72-76-80} Bobbles and 6 dc.

Row 17: Ch 3, turn; dc in next 2 dc, ch 1, skip next Bobble, ★ 3 dc in next Cluster, ch 1, skip next Bobble; repeat from ★ across to last 3 dc, dc in last 3 dc: 165{177-189-207}{219-231-243} dc and 54{58-62-68}{72-76-80} chs.

Row 18: Ch 3, turn; dc in next 2 dc, work Bobble, skip next ch, ★ work Cluster, work Bobble, skip next ch; repeat from ★ across to last 3 dc, dc in last 3 dc: 53{57-61-67}{71-75-79} Clusters, 54{58-62-68}{72-76-80} Bobbles, and 6 dc.

Rows 19-25: Repeat Rows 17 and 18, 3 times; then repeat Row 17 once **more**; do **not** finish off.

BODY
Change to larger size hook.

Row 1: Ch 3, turn; dc in next 2 dc, work Bobble, (skip next ch, work Cluster, work Bobble) 8{9-10-11}{12-13-14} times, (ch 1, work Bobble) 1{1-1-1}{2-2-2} time(s), skip next 10{10-10-11}{11-11-11} 3-dc groups and next ch for armhole, work Cluster, work Bobble, (skip next ch, work Cluster, work Bobble) 16{18-20-22}{24-26-28} times, (ch 1, work Bobble) 1{1-1-1}{2-2-2} time(s), skip next 10{10-10-11}{11-11-11} 3-dc groups and next ch for armhole, ★ work Cluster, work Bobble, skip next ch; repeat from ★ across to last 3 dc, dc in last 3 dc: 33{37-41-45}{49-53-57} Clusters, 36{40-44-48}{54-58-62} Bobbles, and 2{2-2-2}{4-4-4} chs.

Row 2: Ch 3, turn; dc in next 2 dc, ch 1, skip next Bobble, ★ (3 dc in next Cluster, ch 1, skip next Bobble) across to next ch, (3 dc in next ch, ch 1, skip next Bobble) 1{1-1-1}{2-2-2} time(s); repeat from ★ once **more**, (3 dc in next Cluster, ch 1, skip next Bobble) across to last 3 dc, dc in last 3 dc: 111{123-135-147}{165-177-189} dc and 36{40-44-48}{54-58-62} chs.

Row 3: Ch 3, turn; dc in next 2 dc, work Bobble, skip next ch, ★ work Cluster, work Bobble, skip next ch; repeat from ★ across to last 3 dc, skip next ch, dc in last 3 dc: 35{39-43-47}{53-57-61} Clusters, 36{40-44-48}{54-58-62} Bobbles, and 6 dc.

Instructions continued on page 8.

Row 4: Ch 3, turn; dc in next 2 dc, ch 1, skip next Bobble, ★ 3 dc in next Cluster, ch 1, skip next Bobble; repeat from ★ across to last 3 dc, dc in last 3 dc: 111{123-135-147}{165-177-189} dc and 36{40-44-48}{54-58-62} chs.

Repeat Rows 3 and 4 until piece measures approximately 22" (56 cm) from beginning ch, ending by working Row 4.

Last Row: Ch 1, turn; sc in each dc and in each ch across; finish off.

SLEEVE

Sizes Extra Small, Small, Medium, & Large ONLY
Rnd 1: With **right** side facing and using larger size hook, join yarn with slip st in center ch-1 sp at underarm; ch 3, 3 dc in side of next Bobble, work Bobble, skip next ch, ★ work Cluster, work Bobble, skip next ch; repeat from ★ around to last Bobble, 4 dc in side of last Bobble; join with slip st to first dc: 10{10-10-11} Clusters, 11{11-11-12} Bobbles, and 8 dc.

Sizes Extra Large, 2X-Large, & 3X-Large ONLY
Rnd 1: With **right** side facing and using larger size hook, join yarn with slip st in side of center Bobble at underarm; ch 3, 3 dc in same Bobble, work Bobble, YO, insert hook in side of next Bobble, YO and pull up a loop, YO and draw through 2 loops on hook, † YO, insert hook in **same** Bobble, YO and pull up a loop, YO and draw through 2 loops on hook †; repeat from † to † once **more**, YO and draw through all 4 loops on hook **(counts as one Cluster)**, work Bobble, skip next ch, ★ work Cluster, work Bobble, skip next ch; repeat from ★ around to last Bobble, 4 dc in side of last Bobble; join with slip st to first dc: 12 Clusters, 13 Bobbles, and 8 dc.

All Sizes
Rnd 2: Ch 3, turn; dc in next 4 dc, ch 1, skip next Bobble, ★ 3 dc in next Cluster, ch 1, skip next Bobble; repeat from ★ around to last 3 dc, dc in last 3 dc; join with slip st to first dc: 38{38-38-41}{44-44-44} dc and 11{11-11-12}{13-13-13} chs.

Rnd 3: Ch 3, turn; dc in next 3 dc, work Bobble, skip next ch, ★ work Cluster, work Bobble, skip next ch; repeat from ★ around to last 4 dc, dc in last 4 dc; join with slip st to first dc: 10{10-10-11}{12-12-12} Clusters, 11{11-11-12}{13-13-13} Bobbles, and 8 dc.

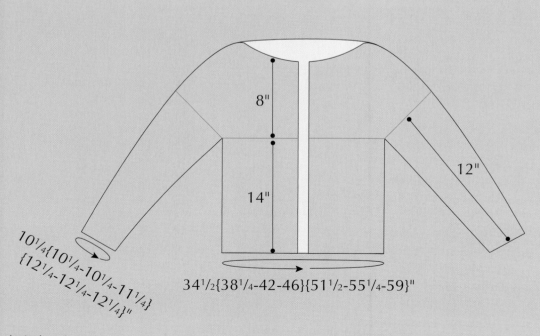

10¼{10¼-10¼-11¼}{12¼-12¼-12¼}"

8"

14"

12"

34½{38¼-42-46}{51½-55¼-59}"

Rnds 4-8: Repeat Rnds 2 and 3 twice, then repeat Rnd 2 once **more**: 38{38-38-41}{44-44-44} dc and 11{11-11-12}{13-13-13} chs.

Rnd 9: Ch 3, turn; dc decrease, dc in next dc, work Bobble, skip next ch, ★ work Cluster, work Bobble, skip next ch; repeat from ★ around to last 4 dc, dc in next dc, dc decrease, dc in last dc; join with slip st to first dc: 10{10-10-11}{12-12-12} Clusters, 11{11-11-12}{13-13-13} Bobbles, and 6 dc.

Rnd 10: Ch 3, turn; dc in next 3 dc, ch 1, skip next Bobble, ★ 3 dc in next Cluster, ch 1, skip next Bobble; repeat from ★ around to last 2 dc, dc in last 2 dc; join with slip st to first dc: 36{36-36-39}{42-42-42} dc and 11{11-11-12}{13-13-13} chs.

Rnd 11: Ch 3, turn; dc in next 2 dc, work Bobble, skip next ch, ★ work Cluster, work Bobble, skip next ch; repeat from ★ around to last 3 dc, dc in last 3 dc; join with slip st to first dc: 10{10-10-11}{12-12-12} Clusters, 11{11-11-12}{13-13-13} Bobbles, and 6 dc.

Rnds 12 and 13: Repeat Rnds 10 and 11.

Rnd 14: Ch 3, turn; dc in next dc, dc decrease, ch 1, skip next Bobble, ★ 3 dc in next Cluster, ch 1, skip next Bobble; repeat from ★ around to last 2 dc, dc decrease; join with slip st to first dc: 34{34-34-37}{40-40-40} dc and 11{11-11-12}{13-13-13} chs.

Work even until Sleeve measures approximately 12" (30.5 cm) from underarm, ending by working a **wrong** side round.

Change to smaller size hook.

Next Rnd: Ch 1, turn; sc in each dc and in each ch around; join with slip st to first sc: 45{45-45-49}{53-53-53} sc.

Last 2 Rnds: Ch 1, turn; sc in each sc around; join with slip st to first sc.

Finish off.

Repeat for second Sleeve.

EDGING

Row 1: With **right** side facing, using smaller size hook, and working in end of rows, join yarn with slip st at lower right front corner; ch 1, work 66 sc evenly spaced across to Row 15 of Yoke, work 11 sc evenly spaced across to top corner: 77 sc.

Row 2: Ch 1, turn; sc in first 5 sc, ch 3, skip next 2 sc (buttonhole made), sc in next 5 sc, **turn**; skip first sc, slip st in next 4 sc, 3 sc in next ch-3 sp, slip st in next 4 sc, 3 sc in last sc; working in free loops of beginning ch across neck edge (**Fig. 2, page 126**), sc in first 3{5-3-3}{2-2-1} ch(s), ★ skip next ch, sc in next 5 chs; repeat from ★ across neck edge; working in end of rows, 3 sc in end of first row, work 11 sc evenly spaced across to end of Row 15, work 66 sc evenly spaced across to lower corner of left front; finish off.

Sew button to left front opposite buttonhole.

Buttons & Shells Jacket

◼◼◼▢ INTERMEDIATE

Size	Finished Chest Measurement
Small	35" (89 cm)
Medium	43$\frac{1}{4}$" (110 cm)
Large	51$\frac{1}{2}$" (131 cm)

Size Note: Instructions are written for size Small with sizes Medium and Large in braces { }. Instructions will be easier to read if you circle all the numbers pertaining to your size. If only one number is given, it applies to all sizes.

MATERIALS

Light Weight Yarn
 [3 ounces, 251 yards
 (85 grams, 230 meters) per skein]:
  {8-10-12} skeins
Crochet hooks, sizes H (5 mm) **and** I (5.5 mm)
  or sizes needed for gauge
Yarn needle
Sewing needle and thread
1$\frac{1}{2}$" (38 mm) Buttons - 4

GAUGE: With larger size hook, in Shell Pattern,
  24 sts = 4" (10 cm);
  14 rows = 4$\frac{1}{4}$" (10.75 cm)

Gauge Swatch: 4$\frac{1}{2}$" (11.5 cm) square
Ch 29.
Row 1: Sc in second ch from hook and in each ch across: 28 sc.

Row 2 (Right side)**:** Ch 3 **(counts as first dc, now and throughout)**, turn; 2 dc in same st, skip next 2 sc, sc in next sc, ★ skip next 2 sc, work Shell in next sc, skip next 2 sc, sc in next sc; repeat from ★ across: 4 Shells.
Rows 3-15: Ch 3, turn; 2 dc in same st, skip next 2 dc, sc in next dc, ★ skip next 2 dc, work Shell in next sc, skip next 2 dc, sc in next dc; repeat from ★ across.

Finish off.

STITCH GUIDE
SHELL
5 Dc in st indicated.

Instructions continued on page 12.

Jacket

Body is worked in one piece from side-to-side, beginning at Left Front.

LEFT FRONT

With larger size hook, ch 89{95-101}.

Row 1: Sc in second ch from hook and in each ch across: 88{94-100} sc.

Row 2 (Right side)**:** Ch 3 **(counts as first dc, now and throughout)**, turn; 2 dc in same st, skip next 2 sc, sc in next sc, ★ skip next 2 sc, work Shell in next sc, skip next 2 sc, sc in next sc; repeat from ★ across: 14{15-16} Shells.

Note: Loop a short piece of yarn around any stitch to mark Row 2 as **right** side.

Rows 3 thru 6{10-14}: Ch 3, turn; 2 dc in same st, skip next 2 dc, sc in next dc, ★ skip next 2 dc, work Shell in next sc, skip next 2 dc, sc in next dc; repeat from ★ across; do **not** finish off.

NECK SHAPING

Row 1 (Increase row)**:** Ch 3, turn; work Shell in same st, skip next 2 dc, sc in next dc, ★ skip next 2 dc, work Shell in next sc, skip next 2 dc, sc in next dc; repeat from ★ across: 15{16-17} Shells.

Row 2: Ch 3, turn; 2 dc in same st, ★ skip next 2 dc, sc in next dc, skip next 2 dc, work Shell in next st; repeat from ★ across.

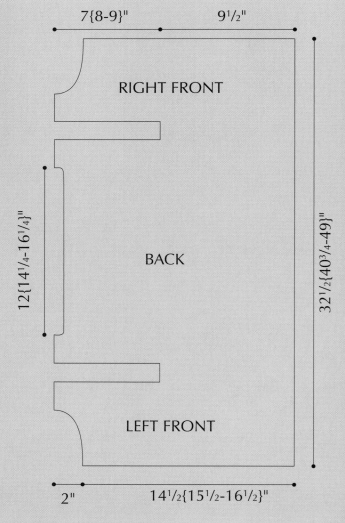

7{8-9}"   9½"

RIGHT FRONT

12{14¼-16¼}"

BACK

32½{40¾-49}"

LEFT FRONT

2"   14½{15½-16½}"

Row 3: Ch 3, turn; 2 dc in same st, skip next dc, sc in next dc, ★ skip next 2 dc, work Shell in next sc, skip next 2 dc, sc in next dc; repeat from ★ across.

Rows 4-6: Ch 3, turn; 2 dc in same st, skip next 2 dc, sc in next dc, ★ skip next 2 dc, work Shell in next sc, skip next 2 dc, sc in next dc; repeat from ★ across.

Rows 7 and 8: Repeat Rows 1 and 2: 16{17-18} Shells.

SHOULDER
Row 1: Ch 3, turn; 2 dc in same st, mark st just worked into to mark beginning of shoulder, skip next dc, sc in next dc, ★ skip next 2 dc, work Shell in next sc, skip next 2 dc, sc in next dc; repeat from ★ across.

Rows 2 thru 7{9-11}: Ch 3, turn; 2 dc in same st, skip next 2 dc, sc in next dc, ★ skip next 2 dc, work Shell in next sc, skip next 2 dc, sc in next dc; repeat from ★ across; do **not** finish off.

ARMHOLE
Row 1: Ch 3, turn; 2 dc in same st, skip next 2 dc, sc in next dc, ★ skip next 2 dc, work Shell in next sc, skip next 2 dc, sc in next dc; repeat from ★ 8 times **more**, leave remaining sts unworked: 9 Shells.

Rows 2 thru 5{7-9}: Ch 3, turn; 2 dc in same st, skip next 2 dc, sc in next dc, ★ skip next 2 dc, work Shell in next sc, skip next 2 dc, sc in next dc; repeat from ★ across; do **not** finish off.

BACK
SHOULDER
Row 1: Ch 45{51-57}, turn; 2 dc in fourth ch from hook (**3 skipped chs count as first dc, now and throughout**), skip next 2 chs, sc in next ch, ★ skip next 2 sts, work Shell in next st, skip next 2 sts, sc in next st; repeat from ★ across: 16{17-18} Shells.

Rows 2 thru 7{9-11}: Ch 3, turn; 2 dc in same st, skip next 2 dc, sc in next dc, ★ skip next 2 dc, work Shell in next sc, skip next 2 dc, sc in next dc; repeat from ★ across; do **not** finish off.

NECK SHAPING
Row 1: Ch 3, turn; 2 dc in same st, skip next 2 dc, sc in next dc, ★ skip next 2 dc, work Shell in next sc, skip next 2 dc, sc in next dc; repeat from ★ across to last 6 sts, leave remaining sts unworked: 15{16-17} Shells.

Row 2: Ch 3, turn; 2 dc in same st, skip next 2 dc, sc in next dc, ★ skip next 2 dc, work Shell in next sc, skip next 2 dc, sc in next dc; repeat from ★ across.

Repeat Row 2 until piece measures 12{14¼-16¼}"/30.5{36-41.5} cm from beginning of Neck Shaping, ending by working a **right** side row.

Instructions continued on page 14.

SHOULDER

Row 1: Ch 9, turn; 2 dc in fourth ch from hook, skip next 2 chs, sc in next ch, ★ skip next 2 sts, work Shell in next sc, skip next 2 dc, sc in next dc; repeat from ★ across: 16{17-18} Shells.

Rows 2 thru 7{9-11}: Ch 3, turn; 2 dc in same st, skip next 2 dc, sc in next dc, ★ skip next 2 dc, work Shell in next sc, skip next 2 dc, sc in next dc; repeat from ★ across; do **not** finish off.

ARMHOLE

Row 1: Ch 3, turn; 2 dc in same st, skip next 2 dc, sc in next dc, ★ skip next 2 dc, work Shell in next sc, skip next 2 dc, sc in next dc; repeat from ★ 8 times **more**, leave remaining sts unworked: 9 Shells.

Rows 2 thru 5{7-9}: Ch 3, turn; 2 dc in same st, skip next 2 dc, sc in next dc, ★ skip next 2 dc, work Shell in next sc, skip next 2 dc, sc in next dc; repeat from ★ across; do **not** finish off.

RIGHT FRONT
SHOULDER

Row 1: Ch 45{51-57}, turn; 2 dc in fourth ch from hook, skip next 2 chs, sc in next ch, ★ skip next 2 sts, work Shell in next st, skip next 2 sts, sc in next st; repeat from ★ across: 16{17-18} Shells.

Rows 2 thru 7{9-11}: Ch 3, turn; 2 dc in same st, skip next 2 dc, sc in next dc, ★ skip next 2 dc, work Shell in next sc, skip next 2 dc, sc in next dc; repeat from ★ across; do **not** finish off.

NECK SHAPING

Row 1: Ch 3, turn; 2 dc in same st, ★ skip next 2 dc, sc in next dc, skip next 2 dc, work Shell in next sc; repeat from ★ across to last 3 dc, leave remaining dc unworked.

Row 2: Ch 3, turn; skip next dc, sc in next dc, ★ skip next 2 dc, work Shell in next sc, skip next 2 dc, sc in next dc; repeat from ★ across.

Row 3: Ch 3, turn; 2 dc in same st, skip next 2 dc, sc in next dc, ★ skip next 2 dc, work Shell in next sc, skip next 2 dc, sc in next dc; repeat from ★ to last 4 sts, skip next 2 dc, 3 dc in next sc, leave remaining dc unworked: 15{16-17} Shells.

Row 4: Ch 1, turn; skip first 3 dc, work Shell in next sc, skip next 2 dc, sc in next dc, ★ skip next 2 dc, work Shell in next sc, skip next 2 dc, sc in next dc; repeat from ★ across: 16{17-18} Shells.

Row 5: Ch 3, turn; 2 dc in same st, skip next 2 dc, sc in next dc, ★ skip next 2 dc, work Shell in next sc, skip next 2 dc, sc in next dc; repeat from ★ across to last 2 dc, leave remaining dc unworked: 15{16-17} Shells.

Row 6: Ch 3, turn; 2 dc in same st, skip next 2 dc, sc in next dc, ★ skip next 2 dc, work Shell in next sc, skip next 2 dc, sc in next dc; repeat from ★ across.

Rows 7-10: Repeat Rows 1-4: 14{15-16} Shells.

Rows 11 thru 13{17-21}: Ch 3, turn; 2 dc in same st, skip next 2 dc, sc in next dc, ★ skip next 2 dc, work Shell in next sc, skip next 2 dc, sc in next dc; repeat from ★ across.

Row 14{18-22}: Ch 1, turn; sc in each st across; finish off: 88{94-100} sc.

SLEEVE (Make 2)
With larger size hook, ch 65{71-77}.

Row 1: Sc in second ch from hook and in each ch across: 64{70-76} sc.

Row 2 (Right side)**:** Ch 3, turn; 2 dc in same st, skip next 2 sc, sc in next sc, ★ skip next 2 sc, work Shell in next sc, skip next 2 sc, sc in next sc; repeat from ★ across: 10{11-12} Shells.

Note: Mark Row 2 as **right** side.

Rows 3-17: Ch 3, turn; 2 dc in same st, skip next 2 dc, sc in next dc, ★ skip next 2 dc, work Shell in next sc, skip next 2 dc, sc in next dc; repeat from ★ across.

Row 18: Ch 3, turn; work Shell in same st, skip next 2 dc, sc in next dc, ★ skip next 2 dc, work Shell in next sc, skip next 2 dc, sc in next dc; repeat from ★ across: 11{12-13} Shells.

Row 19: Ch 3, turn; work Shell in same st, skip next 2 dc, sc in next dc, ★ skip next 2 dc, work Shell in next sc, skip next 2 dc, sc in next dc; repeat from ★ across to last 3 dc, skip next 2 dc, dc in last dc.

Row 20: Ch 1, turn; sc in first dc, work Shell in next sc, skip next 2 dc, sc in next dc, ★ skip next 2 dc, work Shell in next sc, skip next 2 dc, sc in next dc; repeat from ★ across to last 3 dc, skip next 2 dc, dc in last dc.

Row 21: Ch 1, turn; sc in first dc, work Shell in next sc, skip next 2 dc, sc in next dc, ★ skip next 2 dc, work Shell in next sc, skip next 2 dc, sc in next dc; repeat from ★ across to last 3 sts, skip next 2 dc, 3 dc in last sc.

Row 22: Ch 3, turn; 2 dc in same st, skip next dc, sc in next dc, work Shell in next sc, skip next 2 dc, sc in next dc, ★ skip next 2 dc, work Shell in next sc, skip next 2 dc, sc in next dc; repeat from ★ across to last 3 sts, skip next 2 dc, 3 dc in last sc.

Instructions continued on page 16.

14¹/₂{15¹/₂-16¹/₂}"

17"

10¹/₂{11¹/₂-12¹/₂}"

Row 23: Ch 3, turn; 2 dc in same st, skip next dc, sc in next dc, work Shell in next sc, skip next 2 dc, sc in next dc, ★ skip next 2 dc, work Shell in next sc, skip next 2 dc, sc in next dc; repeat from ★ across: 12{13-14} Shells.

Rows 24-31: Ch 3, turn; 2 dc in same st, skip next 2 dc, sc in next dc, ★ skip next 2 dc, work Shell in next sc, skip next 2 dc, sc in next dc; repeat from ★ across.

Rows 32-37: Repeat Rows 18-23:14{15-16} Shells.

Row 38: Ch 3, turn; 2 dc in same st, skip next 2 dc, sc in next dc, ★ skip next 2 dc, work Shell in next sc, skip next 2 dc, sc in next dc; repeat from ★ across.

Repeat Row 38 until piece measures approximately 17" (43 cm) from beginning ch.

Finish off leaving a long end for sewing.

FINISHING
Whipstitch shoulder seams *(Fig. 7, page 127)*.

COLLAR
Row 1: With **right** side facing, larger size hook, and working in end of rows, join yarn with sc in last row of Right Front *(see Joining With Sc, page 125)*; work 117{129-141} sc evenly spaced across: 118{130-142} sc.

Row 2: Ch 3, turn; 2 dc in same st, skip next 2 sc, sc in next sc, ★ skip next 2 sc, work Shell in next sc, skip next 2 sc, sc in next sc; repeat from ★ across: 19{21-23} Shells.

Rows 3-14: Ch 3, turn; 2 dc in same st, skip next 2 dc, sc in next dc, ★ skip next 2 dc, work Shell in next sc, skip next 2 dc, sc in next dc; repeat from ★ across.

Finish off.

Row 15: With **wrong** side facing, join yarn with sc in first dc on Row 14; sc in next dc and in each st across; finish off.

RIBBING
BOTTOM
With smaller size hook, ch 15.

Row 1: Sc in second ch from hook and in each ch across: 14 sc.

Row 2: Ch 1, turn; slip st in Front Loop Only of each sc across (*Fig. 1, page 125*).

Row 3: Ch 1, turn; slip st in Front Loop Only of each slip st across.

Repeat Row 3 until piece relaxed measures approximately 3" (7.5 cm) less than Jacket bottom.

Finish off.

Pin to bottom edge of Jacket; then sew in place.

LEFT FRONT
Work same as Bottom Ribbing until piece relaxed measures approximately 1½" (4 cm) less than front edge of Left Front, including Collar.

RIGHT FRONT
With smaller size hook, ch 15.

Row 1: Sc in second ch from hook and in each ch across: 14 sc.

Row 2: Ch 1, turn; slip st in Front Loop Only of each sc across.

Row 3: Ch 1, turn; slip st in Front Loop Only of each slip st across.

Place first buttonhole 1½" (4 cm) from beginning as follows:
Buttonhole Row 1: Ch 1, turn; working in Front Loops Only, slip st in first 5 sts, ch 4, skip next 4 sts (buttonhole made), slip st in last 5 sts.

Buttonhole Row 2: Ch 1, turn; working in Front Loops Only, slip st in first 5 sts, 4 sc in next ch-4 sp, slip st in last 5 sts.

Continue in Ribbing pattern and work buttonhole rows every 5" (12.5 cm) 3 times **more**.

Work even until Right Front Ribbing measures same as Left Front Ribbing.

Finish off.

Sew Left and Right Front Ribbing pieces to Jacket.

COLLAR
Row 1: With **right** side facing, smaller size hook, and working in Front Loops Only, join yarn with slip st in first slip st on Right Front; slip in each st across.

Rows 2-6: Ch 1, turn; slip st in Front Loop Only of each slip st across.

Finish off.

SLEEVE
Row 1: With **right** side facing, smaller size hook, and working in free loops of beginning ch (*Fig. 2, page 126*), join yarn with sc in first ch; sc in each ch across: 64{70-76} sts.

Row 2: Ch 1, turn; slip st in Front Loop Only of each sc across.

Rows 3-8: Ch 1, turn; slip st in Front Loop Only of each slip st across.

Finish off.

Weave Sleeve seams (*Fig. 6, page 127*).

Weave Sleeves to Jacket.

Sew buttons to Left Front opposite the buttonholes.

Puff-Sleeved Cardigan

◧■□□ EASY +

Size	Finished Chest Measurement	
Extra Small	46"	(117 cm)
Small	49"	(124.5 cm)
Medium	55"	(139.5 cm)
Large	60"	(152.5 cm)
Extra Large	65¹/₂"	(166.5 cm)
2X-Large	68¹/₂"	(174 cm)

Size Note: Instructions are written with sizes Extra Small, Small, and Medium in first set of braces { } and sizes Large, Extra Large, and 2X-Large in second set of braces. Instructions will be easier to read if you circle all the numbers pertaining to your size. If only one number is given, it applies to all sizes.

MATERIALS

Medium Weight Yarn
  [1.75 ounces, 108 yards
  (50 grams, 100 meters) per ball]:
    {14-14-15}{16-17-18} balls
Crochet hook, size H (5 mm) **or** size needed for gauge
Yarn needle
Sewing needle and thread
⁵/₈" (16 mm) Buttons - 8

GAUGE: In rib pattern,
        18 sc and 18 rows = 4" (10 cm)
        In Body pattern,
        17 sts = 4" (10 cm);
        8 rows = 3" (7.5 cm)

Gauge Swatches:
In rib pattern, 4" (10 cm) square
Ch 19.
Row 1: Sc in second ch from hook and in each ch across: 18 sc.
Rows 2-18: Ch 1, turn; sc in Back Loop Only of each sc across **(Fig. 1, page 125)**.
Finish off.

In Body pattern, 4"w x 3"h (10 cm x 7.5 cm)
Ch 20.
Row 1: Sc in second ch from hook, ★ skip next 2 chs, (sc, 2 dc) in next ch; repeat from ★ across to last 3 chs, skip next 2 chs, sc in last ch: 17 sts.
Row 2: Ch 3 **(counts as first dc)**, turn; dc in next dc and in each st across.
Row 3: Ch 1, turn; sc in first dc, (sc, 2 dc) in next dc, ★ skip next 2 dc, (sc, 2 dc) in next dc; repeat from ★ across to last 3 dc, skip next 2 dc, sc in next dc.
Rows 4-8: Repeat Rows 2 and 3 twice, then repeat Row 2 once **more**.

STITCH GUIDE

BEGINNING DECREASE
Pull up a loop in each of first 2 sts, YO and draw through all 3 loops on hook **(counts as one sc)**.
DECREASE
Pull up a loop in each of next 2 sts, YO and draw through all 3 loops on hook **(counts as one sc)**.

Instructions continued on page 20.

Body is worked in one piece from side-to-side, beginning at Left Front.

LEFT FRONT
Ch {62-62-66}{66-70-70}.

Row 1: Sc in second ch from hook and in next {11-11-12}{12-13-13} chs, (sc, 2 dc) in next ch, ★ skip next 2 chs, (sc, 2 dc) in next ch; repeat from ★ across to last 3 chs, skip next 2 chs, sc in last ch: {61-61-65}{65-69-69} sts.

Row 2 (Right side)**:** Ch 3 **(counts as first dc, now and throughout)**, turn; dc in next {48-48-51} {51-54-54} sts, sc in Back Loop Only of last {12-12-13}{13-14-14} sc **(Fig. 1, page 125)**.

Note: Loop a short piece of yarn around any stitch to mark Row 2 as **right** side.

Row 3: Ch 1, turn; sc in Back Loop Only of first {12-12-13}{13-14-14} sc, working in **both** loops, (sc, 2 dc) in next dc, ★ skip next 2 dc, (sc, 2 dc) in next dc; repeat from ★ across to last 3 dc, skip next 2 dc, sc in last dc.

Row 4: Ch 3, turn; dc in **both** loops of next {48-48-51}{51-54-54} sts, sc in Back Loop Only of last {12-12-13}{13-14-14} sc.

Repeat Rows 3 and 4, {0-1-2}{2-3-3} time(s) **(see Zeros, page 125)**.

Do **not** finish off.

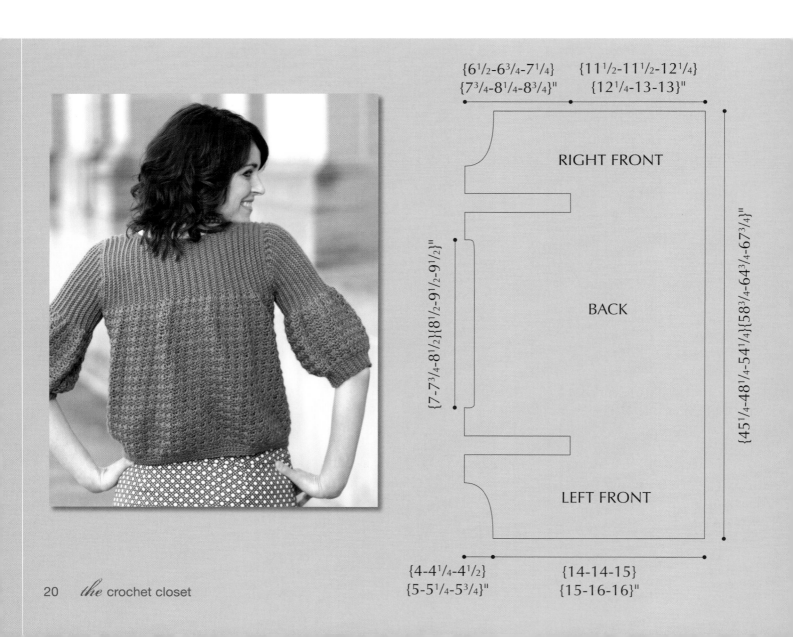

{6¹/₂-6³/₄-7¹/₄} {11¹/₂-11¹/₂-12¹/₄}
{7³/₄-8¹/₄-8³/₄}" {12¹/₄-13-13}"

RIGHT FRONT

BACK

LEFT FRONT

{7-7³/₄-8¹/₂}{8¹/₂-9¹/₂-9¹/₂}"

{45¹/₄-48¹/₄-54¹/₄}{58³/₄-64³/₄-67³/₄}"

{4-4¹/₄-4¹/₂} {14-14-15}
{5-5¹/₄-5³/₄}" {15-16-16}"

NECK SHAPING

Row 1: Ch 1, turn; working in Back Loops Only, 2 sc in each of first 2 sc, sc in next {10-10-11} {11-12-12} sc, working in **both** loops, (sc, 2 dc) in next dc, ★ skip next 2 dc, (sc, 2 dc) in next dc; repeat from ★ across to last 3 dc, skip next 2 dc, sc in last dc: {63-63-67}{67-71-71} sts.

Row 2: Ch 3, turn; dc in **both** loops of next {48-48-51}{51-54-54} sts, place marker before next st *(see Markers, page 125)*, working in Back Loops Only, sc in next {12-12-13}{13-14-14} sc, 2 sc in each of last 2 sc: {65-65-69} {69-73-73} sts.

Move marker up after each row is complete.

Row 3: Ch 1, turn; working in Back Loops Only, 2 sc in first sc, sc in each sc across to marker, working in **both** loops, (sc, 2 dc) in next dc, ★ skip next 2 dc, (sc, 2 dc) in next dc; repeat from ★ across to last 3 dc, skip next 2 dc, sc in last dc: {66-66-70}{70-74-74} sts.

Row 4 (Increase row): Ch 3, turn; dc in **both** loops of next dc and each st across to marker, working in Back Loops Only, sc in each sc across to last sc, 2 sc in last sc: {67-67-71}{71-75-75} sts.

Rows 5-10: Repeat Rows 3 and 4, 3 times: {73-73-77}{77-81-81} sts.

Row 11: Ch {7-9-10}{12-13-15}, turn; sc in second ch from hook and in each ch across, sc in Back Loop Only of each sc across to marker, working in **both** loops, (sc, 2 dc) in next dc, ★ skip next 2 dc, (sc, 2 dc) in next dc; repeat from ★ across to last 3 dc, skip next 2 dc, sc in last dc: {79-81-86}{88-93-95} sts.

Row 12: Ch 3, turn; dc in **both** loops of next dc and each st across to marker, sc in Back Loop Only of each sc across.

Row 13: Ch 1, turn; sc in Back Loop Only of each sc across to marker, working in **both** loops, (sc, 2 dc) in next dc, ★ skip next 2 dc, (sc, 2 dc) in next dc; repeat from ★ across to last 3 dc, skip next 2 dc, sc in last dc.

Rows 14 thru {23-23-25}{27-29-31}: Repeat Rows 12 and 13, {5-5-6}{7-8-9} times.

ARMHOLE SHAPING

Row 1: Ch 3, turn; dc in **both** loops of next dc and each st across to marker, leave remaining sts unworked: {49-49-52}{52-55-55} dc.

Row 2: Ch 1, turn; (sc, 2 dc) in first dc, ★ skip next 2 dc, (sc, 2 dc) in next dc; repeat from ★ across to last 3 dc, skip next 2 dc, sc in last dc.

Row 3: Ch 3, turn; dc in next dc and in each st across.

Repeat Rows 2 and 3, {1-1-1}{2-2-2} time(s).

Do **not** finish off.

BACK

Row 1: Ch {31-33-35}{37-39-41}, turn; sc in second ch from hook and in each ch across, place marker before next st, (sc, 2 dc) in next dc, ★ skip next 2 dc, (sc, 2 dc) in next dc; repeat from ★ across to last 3 dc, skip next 2 dc, sc in last dc: {79-81-86}{88-93-95} sts.

Row 2: Ch 3, turn; dc in **both** loops of next dc and each st across to marker, sc in Back Loop Only of each sc across.

Row 3: Ch 1, turn; sc in Back Loop Only of each sc across to marker, working in **both** loops, (sc, 2 dc) in next dc, ★ skip next 2 dc, (sc, 2 dc) in next dc; repeat from ★ across to last 3 dc, skip next 2 dc, sc in last dc.

Rows 4 thru {13-13-15}{17-19-21}: Repeat Rows 2 and 3, {5-5-6}{7-8-9} times.

LEFT NECK SHAPING

Row 1 (Decrease row): Ch 3, turn; dc in **both** loops of next dc and each st across to marker, working in Back Loops Only, sc in each sc across to last 2 sc, decrease: {78-80-85}{87-92-94} sts.

Instructions continued on page 22.

Row 2 (Decrease row)**:** Ch 1, turn; working in Back Loops Only, work beginning decrease, sc in each sc across to marker, working in **both** loops, (sc, 2 dc) in next dc, ★ skip next 2 dc, (sc, 2 dc) in next dc; repeat from ★ across to last 3 dc, skip next 2 dc, sc in last dc: {77-79-84}{86-91-93} sts.

Rows 3-5: Repeat Rows 1 and 2 once, then repeat Row 1 once **more**: {74-76-81}{83-88-90} sts.

Row 6: Ch 1, turn; sc in Back Loop Only of each sc across to marker, working in **both** loops, (sc, 2 dc) in next dc, ★ skip next 2 dc, (sc, 2 dc) in next dc; repeat from ★ across to last 3 dc, skip next 2 dc, sc in last dc.

Row 7: Ch 3, turn; dc in **both** loops of next dc and each st across to marker, sc in Back Loop Only of each sc across.

Repeat Rows 6 and 7, {9-11-13}{13-15-15} times; then repeat Row 6 once **more**.

RIGHT NECK SHAPING
Row 1 (Increase row)**:** Ch 3, turn; dc in **both** loops of next dc and each st across to marker, sc in Back Loop Only of each sc across to last sc, 2 sc in last sc: {75-77-82}{84-89-91} sts.

Row 2 (Increase row)**:** Ch 1, turn; working in Back Loops Only, 2 sc in first sc, sc in each sc across to marker, working in **both** loops, (sc, 2 dc) in next dc, ★ skip next 2 dc, (sc, 2 dc) in next dc; repeat from ★ across to last 3 dc, skip next 2 dc, sc in last dc: {76-78-83}{85-90-92} sts.

Rows 3-5: Repeat Rows 1 and 2 once, then repeat Row 1 once **more**: {79-81-86}{88-93-95} sts.

Row 6: Ch 1, turn; sc in Back Loop Only of each sc across to marker, working in **both** loops, (sc, 2 dc) in next dc, ★ skip next 2 dc, (sc, 2 dc) in next dc; repeat from ★ across to last 3 dc, skip next 2 dc, sc in last dc.

Row 7: Ch 3, turn; dc in **both** loops of next dc and each st across to marker, sc in Back Loop Only of each sc across.

Rows 8 thru {18-18-20}{22-24-26}: Repeat Rows 6 and 7, {5-5-6}{7-8-9} times; then repeat Row 6 once **more**.

ARMHOLE SHAPING
Row 1: Ch 3, turn; dc in **both** loops of next dc and each st across to marker, remove marker and leave remaining sc unworked: {49-49-52}{52-55-55} dc.

Row 2: Ch 1, turn; (sc, 2 dc) in first dc, ★ skip next 2 dc, (sc, 2 dc) in next dc; repeat from ★ across to last 3 dc, skip next 2 dc, sc in last dc.

Row 3: Ch 3, turn; dc in next dc and in each st across.

Repeat Rows 2 and 3, {1-1-1}{2-2-2} times.

Do **not** finish off.

RIGHT FRONT
Row 1: Ch {31-33-35}{37-39-41}, turn; sc in second ch from hook and in each ch across, place marker before next st, (sc, 2 dc) in next dc, ★ skip next 2 dc, (sc, 2 dc) in next dc; repeat from ★ across to last 3 dc, skip next 2 dc, sc in last dc: {79-81-86}{88-93-95} sts.

Row 2: Ch 3, turn; dc in **both** loops of next dc and each st across to marker, sc in Back Loop Only of each sc across.

Row 3: Ch 1, turn; sc in Back Loop Only of each sc across to marker, working in **both** loops, (sc, 2 dc) in next dc, ★ skip next 2 dc, (sc, 2 dc) in next dc; repeat from ★ across to last 3 dc, skip next 2 dc, sc in last dc.

Rows 4 thru {13-13-15}{17-19-21}: Repeat Rows 2 and 3, {5-5-6}{7-8-9} times.

NECK SHAPING
Row 1: Ch 3, turn; dc in **both** loops of next dc and each st across to marker, sc in Back Loop Only of each sc across to last {6-8-9}{11-12-14} sc, leave remaining sc unworked: {73-73-77}{77-81-81} sts.

Row 2 (Decrease row)**:** Ch 1, turn; working in Back Loops Only, work beginning decrease, sc in each sc across to marker, working in **both** loops, (sc, 2 dc) in next dc, ★ skip next 2 dc, (sc, 2 dc) in next dc; repeat from ★ across to last 3 dc, skip next 2 dc, sc in last dc: {72-72-76}{76-80-80} sts.

Row 3 (Decrease row)**:** Ch 3, turn; dc in **both** loops of next dc and each st across to marker, working in Back Loops Only, sc in each sc across to last 2 sc, decrease: {71-71-75}{75-79-79} sts.

Rows 4-9: Repeat Rows 2 and 3, 3 times: {65-65-69}{69-73-73}.

Row 10: Ch 1, turn; working in Back Loops Only, decrease twice, sc in each sc across to marker, working in **both** loops, (sc, 2 dc) in next dc, ★ skip next 2 dc, (sc, 2 dc) in next dc; repeat from ★ across to last 3 dc, skip next 2 dc, sc in last dc: {63-63-67}{67-71-71} sts.

Row 11: Ch 3, turn; dc in **both** loops of next dc and each st across to marker, working in Back Loops Only, sc in each sc across to last 4 sc, decrease twice: {61-61-65}{65-69-69} sts.

Row 12: Ch 1, turn; sc in Back Loop Only of each sc across to marker, working in **both** loops, (sc, 2 dc) in next dc, ★ skip next 2 dc, (sc, 2 dc) in next dc; repeat from ★ across to last 3 dc, skip next 2 dc, sc in last dc.

Row 13: Ch 3, turn; dc in **both** loops of next dc and in each st across to marker, sc in Back Loop Only of each sc across.

Repeat Rows 12 and 13, {0-1-2}{2-3-3} time(s), then repeat Row 12 once **more**.

Finish off.

SLEEVE (Make 2)
Sleeve is worked in one piece from side-to-side.

Ch 46.

Row 1: Sc in second ch from hook and in next 13 chs, (sc, 2 dc) in next ch, ★ skip next 2 chs, (sc, 2 dc) in next ch; repeat from ★ 6 times **more**, skip next 2 chs, sc in last 7 chs: 45 sts.

Row 2 (Right side)**:** Ch 1, turn; sc in Back Loop Only of first 7 sc, dc in **both** loops of next 24 sts, sc in Back Loop Only of last 14 sc.

Note: Mark Row 2 as **right** side.

Row 3: Ch 1, turn; sc in Back Loop Only of first 14 sc, working in **both** loops, (sc, 2 dc) in next dc, ★ skip next 2 dc, (sc, 2 dc) in next dc; repeat from ★ 6 times **more**, skip next 2 dc, sc in Back Loop Only of last 7 sc.

Rows 4-6: Repeat Rows 2 and 3 once, then repeat Row 2 once **more**.

Do **not** finish off.

CAP SHAPING
First Side
Row 1: Ch 1, turn; working in Back Loops Only, 2 sc in each of first {2-2-3}{3-3-3} sc, sc in next {12-12-11}{11-11-11} sc, place marker before next st, working in **both** loops, (sc, 2 dc) in next dc, ★ skip next 2 dc, (sc, 2 dc) in next dc; repeat from ★ 6 times **more**, skip next 2 dc, sc in Back Loop Only of last 7 sc: {47-47-48}{48-48-48} sts.

Row 2 (Increase row)**:** Ch 1, turn; sc in Back Loop Only of first 7 sc, dc in **both** loops of next dc and each st across to marker, working in Back Loops Only, sc in each sc across to last {2-2-3}{3-3-3} sc, 2 sc in each of last {2-2-3}{3-3-3} sc: {49-49-51}{51-51-51} sts.

Instructions continued on page 24.

Row 3 (Increase row): Ch 1, turn; working in Back Loops Only, 2 sc in each of first {2-2-3}{3-3-3} sc, sc in each sc across to marker, working in **both** loops, (sc, 2 dc) in next dc, ★ skip next 2 dc, (sc, 2 dc) in next dc; repeat from ★ 6 times **more**, skip next 2 dc, sc in Back Loop Only of last 7 sc: {51-51-54}{54-54-54} sts.

Rows 4-6: Repeat Rows 2 and 3 once, then repeat Row 2 once **more**: {57-57-63}{63-63-63} sts.

Row 7 (Increase row): Ch 1, turn; working in Back Loops Only, 2 sc in first sc, sc in each sc across to marker, working in **both** loops, (sc, 2 dc) in next dc, ★ skip next 2 dc, (sc, 2 dc) in next dc; repeat from ★ 6 times **more**, skip next 2 dc, sc in Back Loop Only of last 7 sc: {58-58-64}{64-64-64} sts.

Row 8 (Increase row): Ch 1, turn; sc in Back Loop Only of first 7 sc, dc in **both** loops of next dc and each st across to marker, working in Back Loops Only, sc in each sc across to last sc, 2 sc in last sc: {59-59-65}{65-65-65} sts.

Rows 9-14: Repeat Rows 7 and 8, 3 times: {65-65-71}{71-71-71} sts.

Row 15: Ch 1, turn; sc in Back Loop Only of each sc across to marker, working in **both** loops, (sc, 2 dc) in next dc, ★ skip next 2 dc, (sc, 2 dc) in next dc; repeat from ★ 6 times **more**, skip next 2 dc, sc in Back Loop Only of last 7 sc.

Row 16: Ch 1, turn; sc in Back Loop Only of first 7 sc, dc in **both** loops of next dc and each st across to marker, sc in Back Loop Only of each sc across.

Repeat Rows 15 and 16, {2-2-4}{4-6-6} times.

Second Side
Row 1 (Decrease row): Ch 1, turn; working in Back Loops Only, work beginning decrease, sc in each sc across to marker, working in **both** loops, (sc, 2 dc) in next dc, ★ skip next 2 dc, (sc, 2 dc) in next dc; repeat from ★ 6 times **more**, skip next 2 dc, sc in Back Loop Only of last 7 sc: {64-64-70}{70-70-70} sts.

Row 2 (Decrease row): Ch 1, turn; sc in Back Loop Only of first 7 sc, dc in **both** loops of next dc in and each st across to marker, working in Back Loops Only, sc in each sc across to last 2 sc, decrease: {63-63-69}{69-69-69} sts.

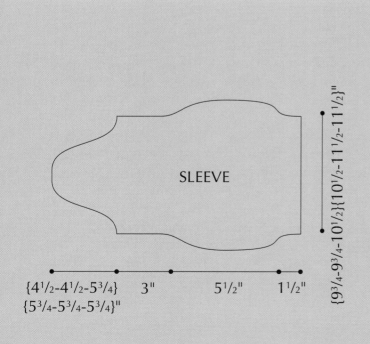

SLEEVE

{4½-4½-5¾}
{5¾-5¾-5¾}"   3"   5½"   1½"

{9¾-9¾-10½}{10½-11½-11½}"

Rows 3-8: Repeat Rows 1 and 2, 3 times: {57-57-63}{63-63-63} sts.

Row 9 (Decrease row)**:** Ch 1, turn; working in Back Loops Only, decrease {2-2-3}{3-3-3} times, sc in each sc across to marker, working in **both** loops, (sc, 2 dc) in next dc, ★ skip next 2 dc, (sc, 2 dc) in next dc; repeat from ★ 6 times **more**, skip next 2 dc, sc in Back Loop Only of last 7 sc: {55-55-60}{60-60-60} sts.

Row 10 (Decrease row)**:** Ch 1, turn; sc in Back Loop Only of first 7 sc, dc in **both** loops of next dc and each st across to marker, working in Back Loops Only, sc in each sc across to last {4-4-6}{6-6-6} sc, decrease {2-2-3}{3-3-3} times: {53-53-57}{57-57-57} sts.

Rows 11-14: Repeat Rows 9 and 10 twice: 45 sts.

Row 15: Ch 1, turn; sc in Back Loop Only of each sc across to marker, working in **both** loops, (sc, 2 dc) in next dc, ★ skip next 2 dc, (sc, 2 dc) in next dc; repeat from ★ 6 times **more**, skip next 2 dc, sc in Back Loop Only of last 7 sc.

Row 16: Ch 1, turn; sc in Back Loop Only of first 7 sc, dc in **both** loops of next dc and each st across to marker, sc in Back Loop Only of each sc across.

Rows 17-20: Repeat Rows 15 and 16 twice.

Finish off.

FINISHING
Whipstitch shoulder seams (**Fig. 7, page 127**).

BOTTOM EDGING
Row 1: With **right** side facing, join yarn with slip st in bottom corner of Left Front; ch 1, working in end of rows, sc evenly across bottom edge to corner of Right Front.

Rows 2-5: Ch 1, turn; sc in each sc across.

Do **not** finish off.

RIGHT FRONT EDGING
Row 1: Ch 1, sc in end of each row on Bottom Edging and in each st across last row of Right Front: {66-66-70}{70-74-74} sc.

Row 2 (Buttonhole row)**:** Ch 1, turn; sc in first {2-2-3}{3-4-4} sc, ★ ch 1, skip next sc (buttonhole made), sc in next 4 sc, ch 1, skip next sc, sc in next {12-12-13}{13-14-14} sc; repeat from ★ 2 times **more**, (ch 1, skip next sc, sc in next 4 sc) twice: {58-58-62}{62-66-66} sc and 8 ch-1 sps.

Row 3: Ch 1, turn; sc in each sc and in each ch-1 sp across: {66-66-70}{70-74-74} sc.

Rows 4 and 5: Ch 1, turn; sc in each sc across.

Finish off.

LEFT FRONT EDGING
Row 1: With **right** side facing, join yarn with slip st in top corner of Left Front; ch 1, sc in free loop of each ch across Left Front and in end of each row on Bottom Edging: {66-66-70}{70-74-74} sc.

Rows 2-5: Ch 1, turn; sc in each sc across.

Finish off.

NECK EDGING
Row 1: With **right** side facing, join yarn with slip st in top corner of Right Front; ch 1, sc evenly across end of rows along neck edge to top corner of Left Front.

Rows 2 and 3: Ch 1, turn; sc in each sc across, decreasing as necessary to keep piece lying flat.

Finish off.

Weave Sleeve seams (**Fig. 6, page 127**).

Weave Sleeves to Cardigan.

Sew buttons to Left Front opposite buttonholes.

Double-Up Jacket

◧◼◻◻ **EASY +**

Size	Finished Chest Measurement (buttoned)
Small	36½" (92.5 cm)
Medium	39" (99 cm)
Large	43¾" (111 cm)
Extra Large	48½" (123 cm)
2X-Large	53½" (136 cm)
3X-Large	58" (147.5 cm)

Size Note: Instructions are written with sizes Small, Medium, and Large in first set of braces { } and sizes Extra Large, 2X-Large, and 3X-Large in second set of braces. Instructions will be easier to read if you circle all the numbers pertaining to your size. If only one number is given, it applies to all sizes.

MATERIALS

Medium Weight Yarn
[3 ounces, 150 yards
(85 grams, 137 meters) per skein]:
{10-10-11}{11-12-12} skeins
Crochet hook, size H (5 mm) **or** size needed for gauge
Split-ring markers - 2
Yarn needle
Sewing needle and thread
1" (25 mm) Buttons - 4

GAUGE: In pattern, 14 sts = 4¼" (10.75 cm);
10 rows = 4" (10 cm)

Gauge Swatch: 4¼"w x 4"h (10.75 cm x 10 cm)
Ch 17.
Row 1 (Right side)**:** Dc in fourth ch from hook **(3 skipped chs count as first dc)** and in each ch across: 15 dc.
Row 2: Ch 3 **(counts as first dc, now and throughout)**, turn; dc in next dc, (skip next dc, 2 dc in next dc) across to last 3 dc, skip next dc, dc in last 2 dc: 14 dc.
Rows 3-10: Ch 3, turn; dc in next dc, skip next dc, 2 dc in sp **before** next dc **(Fig. 5, page 126)**, (skip next 2 dc, 2 dc in sp **before** next dc) across to last 3 dc, skip next dc, dc in last 2 dc.
Finish off.

Instructions continued on page 28.

Jacket

Body is worked in one piece to armholes.

BODY
Ch {175-187-203}{219-231-247}.

Row 1 (Right side)**:** Dc in fourth ch from hook **(3 skipped chs count as first dc)** and in each ch across: {173-185-201}{217-229-245} dc.

Note: Loop a short piece of yarn around any stitch to mark Row 1 as **right** side.

Row 2: Ch 3 **(counts as first dc, now and throughout)**, turn; dc in next dc, ★ skip next dc, 2 dc in next dc; repeat from ★ across to last 3 dc, skip next dc, dc in last 2 dc: {172-184-200}{216-228-244} dc.

Rows 3-6: Ch 3, turn; dc in next dc, skip next dc, 2 dc in sp **before** next dc *(Fig. 5, page 126)*, ★ skip next 2 dc, 2 dc in sp **before** next dc; repeat from ★ across to last 3 dc, skip next dc, dc in last 2 dc.

Place split-ring marker in sp **before** {53rd-57th-61st}{65th-67th-71st} dc from each edge to mark decreases and increases. Move markers up after each row is complete.

Row 7 (Decrease row)**:** Ch 3, turn; dc in next dc, skip next dc, 2 dc in sp **before** next dc, ★ (skip next 2 dc, 2 dc in sp **before** next dc) across to within 5 dc of next marker, (skip next 2 dc, dc in sp **before** next dc) 4 times; repeat from ★ once **more**, (skip next 2 dc, 2 dc in sp **before** next dc) across to last 3 dc, skip next dc, dc in last 2 dc: {164-176-192}{208-220-236} dc.

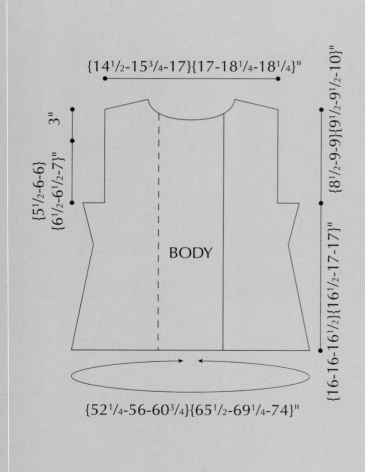

{14¹/₂-15³/₄-17}{17-18¹/₄-18¹/₄}"

3"

{5¹/₂-6-6}{6¹/₂-6¹/₂-7}"

BODY

{8¹/₂-9-9}{9¹/₂-9¹/₂-10}"

{16-16-16¹/₂}{16¹/₂-17-17}"

{52¹/₄-56-60³/₄}{65¹/₂-69¹/₄-74}"

Rows 8-10: Ch 3, turn; dc in next dc, skip next dc, 2 dc in sp **before** next dc, ★ skip next 2 dc, 2 dc in sp **before** next dc; repeat from ★ across to last 3 dc, skip next dc, dc in last 2 dc.

Rows 11-22: Repeat Rows 7-10, 3 times: {140-152-168}{184-196-212} dc.

Rows 23 and 24: Ch 3, turn; dc in next dc, skip next dc, 2 dc in sp **before** next dc, ★ skip next 2 dc, 2 dc in sp **before** next dc; repeat from ★ across to last 3 dc, skip next dc, dc in last 2 dc.

Row 25: Ch 3, turn; dc in next dc, skip next dc, 2 dc in sp **before** next dc, ★ (skip next 2 dc, 2 dc in sp **before** next dc) across to within 3 dc of next marker, (skip next 2 dc, 4 dc in sp **before** next dc) twice; repeat from ★ once **more**, (skip next 2 dc, 2 dc in sp **before** next dc) across to last 3 dc, skip next dc, dc in last 2 dc: {148-160-176}{192-204-220} dc.

Rows 26-30: Ch 3, turn; dc in next dc, skip next dc, 2 dc in sp **before** next dc, ★ skip next 2 dc, 2 dc in sp **before** next dc; repeat from ★ across to last 3 dc, skip next dc, dc in last 2 dc.

Row 31: Ch 3, turn; dc in next dc, skip next dc, 2 dc in sp **before** next dc, ★ (skip next 2 dc, 2 dc in sp **before** next dc) across to within 3 dc of next marker, (skip next 2 dc, 4 dc in sp **before** next dc) twice; repeat from ★ once **more**, (skip next 2 dc, 2 dc in sp **before** next dc) across to last 3 dc, skip next dc, dc in last 2 dc: {156-168-184}{200-212-228} dc.

Work even until Body measures {16-16-16½}{16½-17-17}"/{40.5-40.5-42}{42-43-43} cm from beginning ch, ending by working a **wrong** side row; do **not** remove markers and do **not** finish off.

RIGHT FRONT
ARMHOLE SHAPING

Row 1: Ch 3, turn; dc in next dc, skip next dc, 2 dc in sp **before** next dc, ★ skip next 2 dc, 2 dc in sp **before** next dc; repeat from ★ across to within {5-5-5}{7-9-11} dc of marker, skip next 2 dc, dc in sp **before** next dc, leave remaining sts unworked: {45-49-53}{55-55-57} dc.

Row 2: Ch 3, turn; skip next dc, dc in sp **before** next dc, skip next 2 dc, dc in sp **before** next dc, ★ skip next 2 dc, 2 dc in sp **before** next dc; repeat from ★ across to last 3 dc, skip next dc, dc in last 2 dc: {43-47-51}{53-53-55} dc.

Row 3: Ch 3, turn; dc in next dc, skip next dc, 2 dc in sp **before** next dc, ★ skip next 2 dc, 2 dc in sp **before** next dc; repeat from ★ across to last 4 dc, skip next 2 dc, dc in sp **before** next dc, skip next dc, dc in last dc: {42-46-50}{52-52-54} dc.

Sizes Large, Extra Large, 2X-Large, & 3X-Large ONLY
Row 4: Ch 3, turn; ★ skip next 2 dc, 2 dc in sp **before** next dc; repeat from ★ across to last 3 dc, skip next dc, dc in last 2 dc: {49}{51-51-53} dc.

Row 5: Ch 3, turn; dc in next dc, skip next dc, 2 dc in sp **before** next dc, ★ skip next 2 dc, 2 dc in sp **before** next dc; repeat from ★ across to last 4 dc, skip next 2 dc, dc in sp **before** next dc, skip next dc, dc in last dc: {48}{50-50-52} dc.

Sizes Extra Large, 2X-Large, & 3X-Large ONLY
Repeat Rows 4 and 5, {1-1-2} time(s): 48 dc.

Instructions continued on page 30.

All Sizes
Next Row: Ch 3, turn; dc in next dc, skip next dc, 2 dc in sp **before** next dc, ★ skip next 2 dc, 2 dc in sp **before** next dc; repeat from ★ across to last 3 dc, skip next dc, dc in last 2 dc.

Repeat last row until Armhole measures approximately {5$\frac{1}{2}$-6-6}{6$\frac{1}{2}$-6$\frac{1}{2}$-7}"/ {14-15-15}{16.5-16.5-18} cm, ending by working a **right** side row.

NECK SHAPING
Row 1: Ch 3, turn; dc in next dc, skip next dc, 2 dc in sp **before** next dc, ★ skip next 2 dc, 2 dc in sp **before** next dc; repeat from ★ {5-6-7}{7-7-7} times, skip next 2 dc, dc in sp **before** next dc, leave remaining sts unworked: {17-19-21}{21-21-21} dc.

Row 2: Ch 3, turn; skip next dc, dc in sp **before** next dc, ★ skip next 2 dc, 2 dc in sp **before** next dc; repeat from ★ across to last 3 dc, skip next dc, dc in last 2 dc: {16-18-20}{20-20-20} dc.

Row 3: Ch 3, turn; dc in next dc, skip next dc, 2 dc in sp **before** next dc, ★ skip next 2 dc, 2 dc in sp **before** next dc; repeat from ★ across to last 3 dc, skip next 2 dc, dc in last dc: {15-17-19}{19-19-19} dc.

Row 4: Ch 3, turn; skip next dc, dc in sp **before** next dc, ★ skip next 2 dc, 2 dc in sp **before** next dc; repeat from ★ across to last 3 dc, skip next dc, dc in last 2 dc: {14-16-18}{18-18-18} dc.

Row 5: Ch 3, turn; dc in next dc, skip next dc, 2 dc in sp **before** next dc, ★ skip next 2 dc, 2 dc in sp **before** next dc; repeat from ★ across to last 3 dc, skip next dc, dc in last 2 dc.

Repeat last row until Armhole measures approximately {8$\frac{1}{2}$-9-9}{9$\frac{1}{2}$-9$\frac{1}{2}$-10}"/ {21.5-23-23}{24-24-25.5} cm, ending by working a **wrong** side row.

SHOULDER SHAPING
Row 1: Ch 3, turn; dc in next dc, skip next dc, 2 dc in sp **before** next dc, (skip next 2 dc, 2 dc in sp **before** next dc) {1-2-3}{3-3-3} time(s), skip next 2 dc, (dc, sc) in sp **before** next dc, skip next dc, slip st in next dc, leave remaining sts unworked: {9-11-13}{13-13-13} sts.

Row 2: Turn; skip first st, slip st in next 2 sts, skip next dc, (sc, dc) in sp **before** next dc, (skip next 2 dc, 2 dc in sp **before** next dc) {1-2-3} {3-3-3} time(s), skip next dc, dc in last 2 dc; finish off.

LEFT FRONT
ARMHOLE SHAPING
Row 1: With **right** side facing, skip first {3-3-3}{5-7-9} dc from marker on Body and join yarn with slip st in sp **before** next dc; ch 3, ★ skip next 2 dc, 2 dc in sp **before** next dc; repeat from ★ across to last 3 dc, skip next dc, dc in last 2 dc: {45-49-53}{55-55-57} dc.

Row 2: Ch 3, turn; dc in next dc, skip next dc, 2 dc in sp **before** next dc, ★ skip next 2 dc, 2 dc in sp **before** next dc; repeat from ★ across to last 6 dc, (skip next 2 dc, dc in sp **before** next dc) twice, skip next dc, dc in last dc: {43-47-51}{53-53-55} dc.

Row 3: Ch 3, turn; skip next dc, dc in sp **before** next dc, ★ skip next 2 dc, 2 dc in sp **before** next dc; repeat from ★ across to last 3 dc, skip next dc, dc in last 2 dc: {42-46-50}{52-52-54} dc.

Sizes Large, Extra Large, 2X-Large, & 3X-Large ONLY
Row 4: Ch 3, turn; dc in next dc, skip next dc, 2 dc in sp **before** next dc, ★ skip next 2 dc, 2 dc in sp **before** next dc; repeat from ★ across to last 3 dc, skip next 2 dc, dc in last dc: {49}{51-51-53} dc.

Row 5: Ch 3, turn; skip next dc, dc in sp **before** next dc, ★ skip next 2 dc, 2 dc in sp **before** next dc; repeat from ★ across to last 3 dc, skip next dc, dc in last 2 dc: {48}{50-50-52} dc.

Sizes Extra Large, 2X-Large & 3X-Large ONLY
Repeat Rows 4 and 5, {1-1-2} time(s): 48 dc.

All Sizes
Next Row: Ch 3, turn; dc in next dc, skip next dc, 2 dc in sp **before** next dc, ★ skip next 2 dc, 2 dc in sp **before** next dc; repeat from ★ across to last 3 dc, skip next dc, dc in last 2 dc.

Repeat last row until Armhole measures same as Right Front to Neck Shaping, ending by working a **right** side row.

Finish off.

NECK SHAPING
Row 1: With **wrong** side facing, skip first {11-13-13}{13-13-13} dc and join yarn with slip st in sp **before** next dc; ch 3, ★ skip next 2 dc, 2 dc in sp **before** next dc; repeat from ★ across to last 3 dc, skip next dc, dc in last 2 dc: {17-19-21}{21-21-21} dc.

Row 2: Ch 3, turn; dc in next dc, skip next dc, 2 dc in sp **before** next dc, ★ skip next 2 dc, 2 dc in sp **before** next dc; repeat from ★ across to last 4 dc, skip next 2 dc, dc in sp **before** next dc, skip next dc, dc in last dc: {16-18-20}{20-20-20} dc.

Row 3: Ch 3, turn; ★ skip next 2 dc, 2 dc in sp **before** next dc; repeat from ★ across to last 3 dc, skip next dc, dc in last 2 dc: {15-17-19}{19-19-19} dc.

Row 4: Ch 3, turn; dc in next dc, skip next dc, 2 dc in sp **before** next dc, ★ skip next 2 dc, 2 dc in sp **before** next dc; repeat from ★ across to last 4 dc, skip next 2 dc, dc in sp **before** next dc, skip next dc, dc in last dc: {14-16-18}{18-18-18} dc.

Row 5: Ch 3, turn; dc in next dc, skip next dc, 2 dc in sp **before** next dc, ★ skip next 2 dc, 2 dc in sp **before** next dc; repeat from ★ across to last 3 dc, skip next dc, dc in last 2 dc.

Repeat last row until Armhole measures same as Right Front to Shoulder Shaping, ending by working a **wrong** side row.

SHOULDER SHAPING
Row 1: Turn; slip st in first 6 dc, skip next dc, (sc, dc) in sp **before** next dc, (skip next 2 dc, 2 dc in sp **before** next dc) {2-3-4}{4-4-4} times, skip next dc, dc in last 2 dc.

Row 2: Ch 3, turn; dc in next dc, skip next dc, (2 dc in sp **before** next dc, skip next 2 dc) {1-2-3}{3-3-3} time(s), (dc, sc) in sp **before** next dc, skip next dc, slip st in next dc; finish off.

BACK
ARMHOLE SHAPING
Row 1: With **right** side facing, skip first {6-6-6}{10-14-18} dc and join yarn with slip st in sp **before** next dc; ch 3, ★ skip next 2 dc, 2 dc in sp **before** next dc; repeat from ★ across to within {5-5-5}{7-9-11} dc of next marker, skip next 2 dc, dc in sp **before** next dc, leave remaining sts unworked: {54-58-66}{70-74-78} dc.

Row 2: Ch 3, turn; skip next dc, dc in sp **before** next dc, skip next 2 dc, dc in sp **before** next dc, ★ skip next 2 dc, 2 dc in sp **before** next dc; repeat from ★ across to last 6 dc, (skip next 2 dc, dc in sp **before** next dc) twice, skip next dc, dc in last dc: {50-54-62}{66-70-74} dc.

Row 3: Ch 3, turn; skip next dc, dc in sp **before** next dc, ★ skip next 2 dc, 2 dc in sp **before** next dc; repeat from ★ across to last 4 dc, skip next 2 dc, dc in sp **before** next dc, skip next dc, dc in last dc: {48-52-60}{64-68-72} dc.

Instructions continued on page 32.

Sizes Large, Extra Large, 2X-Large, & 3X-Large ONLY

Row 4: Ch 3, turn; ★ skip next 2 dc, 2 dc in sp **before** next dc; repeat from ★ across to last 3 dc, skip next 2 dc, dc in last dc: {58}{62-66-70} dc.

Row 5: Ch 3, turn; skip next dc, dc in sp **before** next dc, ★ skip next 2 dc, 2 dc in sp **before** next dc; repeat from ★ across to last 4 dc, skip next 2 dc, dc in sp **before** next dc, skip next dc, dc in last dc: {56}{60-64-68} dc.

Sizes Extra Large, 2X-Large & 3X-Large ONLY

Repeat Rows 4 and 5, {1-1-2} time(s): {56-60-60} dc.

All Sizes

Next Row: Ch 3, turn; dc in next dc, skip next dc, 2 dc in sp **before** next dc, ★ skip next 2 dc, 2 dc in sp **before** next dc; repeat from ★ across to last 3 dc, skip next dc, dc in last 2 dc.

Repeat last row until Back measures same as Fronts to Shoulder Shaping, ending by working a **wrong** side row.

RIGHT SHOULDER SHAPING

Row 1: Turn; slip st in first 6 dc, skip next dc, (sc, dc) in sp **before** next dc, (skip next 2 dc, 2 dc in sp **before** next dc) {2-3-4}{4-4-4} times, skip next dc, dc in next 2 dc, leave remaining sts unworked.

Row 2: Ch 3, turn; dc in next dc, skip next dc, (2 dc in sp **before** next dc, skip next 2 dc) {1-2-3}{3-3-3} time(s), (dc, sc) in sp **before** next dc, skip next dc, slip st in next dc; finish off.

LEFT SHOULDER SHAPING

Row 1: With **right** side facing, skip next {20-20-20}{20-24-24} dc from Right Shoulder and join yarn with slip st in next dc; ch 3, dc in next dc, (skip next 2 dc, 2 dc in sp **before** next dc) {1-2-3}{3-3-3} time(s), skip next 2 dc, (dc, sc) in sp **before** next dc, skip next dc, slip st in next dc, leave remaining sts unworked.

Row 2: Turn; skip first st, slip st in next 2 sts, skip next dc, (sc, dc) in sp **before** next dc, (skip next 2 dc, 2 dc in sp **before** next dc) {1-2-3}{3-3-3} time(s), skip next dc, dc in last 2 dc; finish off.

SLEEVE (Make 2)

Ch {51-55-59}{61-63-65}.

Row 1 (Right side)**:** Dc in fourth ch from hook **(3 skipped chs count as first dc)** and in each ch across: {49-53-57}{59-61-63} dc.

Note: Mark Row 1 as **right** side.

Row 2: Ch 3, turn; ★ skip next dc, 2 dc in next dc; repeat from ★ across to last 2 dc, skip next dc, dc in last dc: {48-52-56}{58-60-62} dc.

Rows 3-8: Ch 3, turn; skip next dc, 2 dc in sp **before** next dc, ★ skip next 2 dc, 2 dc in sp **before** next dc; repeat from ★ across to last 2 dc, skip next dc, dc in last dc.

Row 9: Ch 3, turn; skip next dc, dc in sp **before** next dc, ★ skip next 2 dc, 2 dc in sp **before** next dc; repeat from ★ across to last 4 dc, skip next 2 dc, dc in sp **before** next dc, dc in last dc: {46-50-54}{56-58-60} dc.

Rows 10-12: Ch 3, turn; dc in next dc, skip next dc, 2 dc in sp **before** next dc, ★ skip next 2 dc, 2 dc in sp **before** next dc; repeat from ★ across to last 3 dc, skip next dc, dc in last 2 dc.

Row 13: Ch 3, turn; ★ skip next 2 dc, 2 dc in sp **before** next dc; repeat from ★ across to last 3 dc, skip next 2 dc, dc in last dc: {44-48-52}{54-56-58} dc.

Rows 14-17: Ch 3, turn; skip next dc, 2 dc in sp **before** next dc, ★ skip next 2 dc, 2 dc in sp **before** next dc; repeat from ★ across to last 2 dc, skip next dc, dc in last dc.

Row 18: Ch 3, turn; skip next dc, dc in sp **before** next dc, ★ skip next 2 dc, 2 dc in sp **before** next dc; repeat from ★ across to last 4 dc, skip next 2 dc, dc in sp **before** next dc, skip next dc, dc in last dc: {42-46-50}{52-54-56} dc.

Rows 19-30: Ch 3, turn; dc in next dc, skip next dc, 2 dc in sp **before** next dc, ★ skip next 2 dc, 2 dc in sp **before** next dc; repeat from ★ across to last 3 dc, skip next dc, dc in last 2 dc.

Row 31: Ch 3, turn; 2 dc in next dc, skip next dc, 2 dc in sp **before** next dc, ★ skip next 2 dc, 2 dc in sp **before** next dc; repeat from ★ across to last 3 dc, skip next dc, 2 dc in next dc, dc in last dc: {44-48-52}{54-56-58} dc.

Rows 32-35: Ch 3, turn; skip next dc, 2 dc in sp **before** next dc, ★ skip next 2 dc, 2 dc in sp **before** next dc; repeat from ★ across to last 2 dc, skip next dc, dc in last dc.

Instructions continued on page 34.

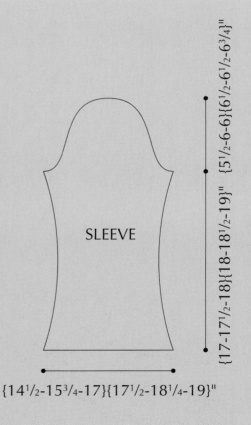

SLEEVE

{5¹/₂-6-6}{6¹/₂-6¹/₂-6³/₄}"

{17-17¹/₂-18}{18-18¹/₂-19}"

{14¹/₂-15³/₄-17}{17¹/₂-18¹/₄-19}"

Row 36: Ch 3, turn; dc in same st, skip next dc, 2 dc in sp **before** next dc, ★ skip next 2 dc, 2 dc in sp **before** next dc; repeat from ★ across to last 2 dc, skip next dc, 2 dc in last dc: {46-50-54}{56-58-60} dc.

Row 37: Ch 3, turn; dc in next dc, skip next dc, 2 dc in sp **before** next dc, ★ skip next 2 dc, 2 dc in sp **before** next dc; repeat from ★ across to last 3 dc, skip next dc, dc in last 2 dc.

Repeat Row 37 until Sleeve measures approximately {17-17$^{1}/_{2}$-18}{18-18$^{1}/_{2}$-19}"/ {43-44.5-45.5}{45.5-47-48.5} cm from beginning ch, ending by working a **wrong** side row.

CAP SHAPING
Row 1: Turn; slip st in first {3-3-3}{5-7-9} dc and in sp **before** next dc, ch 3, ★ skip next 2 dc, 2 dc in sp **before** next dc; repeat from ★ across to last {5-5-5}{7-9-11} dc, skip next 2 dc, dc in sp **before** next dc, leave remaining sts unworked: {40-44-48}{46-44-42} sts.

Sizes Medium, Large, & Extra Large ONLY
Row 2: Ch 3, turn; skip next dc, dc in sp **before** next dc, skip next 2 dc, dc in sp **before** next dc, ★ skip next 2 dc, 2 dc in sp **before** next dc; repeat from ★ across to last 6 dc, (skip next 2 dc, dc in sp **before** next dc) twice, skip next dc, dc in last dc: {40-44}{42} dc.

Size Large ONLY
Repeat Row 2 twice: 36 dc.

All Sizes
First Decrease Row: Ch 3, turn; skip next dc, dc in sp **before** next dc, ★ skip next 2 dc, 2 dc in sp **before** next dc; repeat from ★ across to last 4 dc, skip next 2 dc, dc in sp **before** next dc, skip next dc, dc in last dc: {38-38-34}{40-42-40} dc.

Second Decrease Row: Ch 3, turn; ★ skip next 2 dc, 2 dc in sp **before** next dc; repeat from ★ across to last 3 dc, skip next 2 dc, dc in last dc: {36-36-32}{38-40-38} dc.

Repeat First and Second Decrease Rows, {5-5-4} {6-6-4} times; then repeat First Decrease Row {1-1-1}{0-1-1} time(s) **more (see Zeros, page 125)**: {14-14-14}{14-14-20} dc.

Size 3X-Large ONLY
Next Row: Ch 3, turn; ★ skip next 2 dc, 2 dc in sp **before** next dc; repeat from ★ across to last 3 dc, skip next 2 dc, dc in last dc: 18 dc.

Next Row: Ch 3, turn; skip next dc, 2 dc in sp **before** next dc, ★ skip next 2 dc, 2 dc in sp **before** next dc; repeat from ★ across to last 2 dc, skip next dc, dc in last dc.

Next Row: Repeat First Decrease Row: 16 dc.

Next Row: Ch 3, turn; dc in next dc, skip next dc, 2 dc in sp **before** next dc, ★ skip next 2 dc, 2 dc in sp **before** next dc; repeat from ★ across to last 3 dc, skip next dc, dc in last 2 dc.

Last Row: Repeat Second Decrease Row: 14 dc.

All Sizes
Finish off.

FINISHING
Whipstitch shoulder seams **(Fig. 7, page 127)**.

NECK EDGING
Row 1: With **right** side facing, join yarn with slip st at top right neck edge; ch 1, sc evenly around to left edge.

Row 2: Ch 1, do **not** turn; working from **left** to **right**, work reverse sc in each sc across **(Figs. 8a-d, page 127)**; finish off.

Weave Sleeve seams **(Fig. 6, page 127)**.

Weave Sleeves to Jacket.

Using photo as a guide, sew buttons to Left Front, using spaces between dc on Right Front for buttonholes.

All-Buttoned-Up Vest

■■□□ EASY +

Shown on page 37.

Size	Finished Chest Measurement
Extra Small	32" (81.5 cm)
Small	36" (91.5 cm)
Medium	40" (101.5 cm)
Large	44" (112 cm)
Extra Large	48" (122 cm)
2X-Large	52" (132 cm)

Size Note: Instructions are written with sizes Extra Small, Small, and Medium in first set of braces { } and sizes Large, Extra Large, and 2X-Large in second set of braces. Instructions will be easier to read if you circle all the numbers pertaining to your size. If only one number is given, it applies to all sizes.

MATERIALS
Light Weight Yarn
   [2.5 ounces, 168 yards
   (70 grams, 154 meters) per skein]:
      {6-6-7}{7-8-8} skeins
Crochet hooks, sizes G (4 mm) **and** H (5 mm) **or**
   sizes needed for gauge
Yarn needle
Sewing needle and thread
5/8" (16 mm) Buttons - 6

GAUGE: With larger size hook, in pattern,
   19 sts and 12 rows = 4" (10 cm)

Gauge Swatch: 4" (10 cm) square
With larger size hook, ch 20.
Work Rows 1-4 of Back, page 36, then repeat
Rows 3 and 4, 4 times.
Finish off.

Instructions continued on page 36.

BACK

Back is worked from side-to-side, beginning at left.

LEFT ARMHOLE

With larger size hook, ch 55.

Row 1: Sc in second ch from hook and in each ch across: 54 sc.

Row 2 (Right side)**:** Ch 3 **(counts as first dc, now and throughout)**, turn; working in Back Loops Only **(Fig. 1, page 125)**, dc in next sc and in each sc across.

Note: Loop a short piece of yarn around any stitch to mark Row 2 as **right** side.

Row 3: Ch 1, turn; sc in Front Loop Only of each dc across **(Fig. 1, page 125)**.

Row 4: Ch 3, turn; dc in Back Loop Only of next sc and each sc across.

Repeat Rows 3 and 4, {0-0-1}{1-2-3} time(s) **(see Zeros, page 125)**.

LEFT SHOULDER

Row 1: Ch {40-40-43}{43-45-45}, turn; sc in second ch from hook and in each ch across; sc in Front Loop Only of each dc across: {93-93-96}{96-98-98} sc.

Row 2: Ch 3, turn; dc in Back Loop Only of next sc and each sc across.

Row 3: Ch 1, turn; sc in Front Loop Only of each dc across.

Repeat Rows 2 and 3, {2-3-3}{4-5-5} times.

LEFT NECK SHAPING AND CENTER BACK

Row 1: Ch 3, turn; dc in Back Loop Only of next sc and each sc across to last 5 sc, leave remaining sc unworked: {88-88-91}{91-93-93} dc.

Row 2: Ch 1, turn; sc in Front Loop Only of each dc across.

Row 3: Ch 3, turn; dc in Back Loop Only of next sc and each sc across.

Repeat Rows 2 and 3 until Back measures approximately {12½-13¾-15}{16¼-17¼-18½}"/{32-35-38}{41.5-44-47} cm from beginning ch, ending by working a **right** side row.

RIGHT NECK SHAPING AND SHOULDER

Row 1: Ch 6, turn; sc in second ch from hook and in next 4 chs; sc in Front Loop Only of each dc across: {93-93-96}{96-98-98} sc.

Row 2: Ch 3, turn; dc in Back Loop Only of next sc and each sc across.

Row 3: Ch 1, turn; sc in Front Loop Only of each dc across.

Repeat Rows 2 and 3, {2-3-3}{4-5-5} times.

RIGHT ARMHOLE

Row 1: Ch 3, turn; dc in Back Loop Only of next 53 sc, leave remaining sc unworked: 54 dc.

Row 2: Ch 1, turn; sc in Front Loop Only of each dc across.

Row 3: Ch 3, turn; dc in Back Loop Only of next sc and each sc across.

Row 4: Ch 1, turn; sc in Front Loop Only of each dc across.

Repeat Rows 3 and 4, {0-0-1}{1-2-3} time(s).

Finish off.

Instructions continued on page 38.

Vest

LEFT FRONT

Left Front is worked from side-to-side, beginning at front edge.

With larger size hook, ch 26.

Row 1: Sc in second ch from hook and in each ch across: 25 sc.

Row 2 (Right side - Increase row)**:** Ch 3, turn; working in Back Loops Only, dc in next sc and in each sc across to last sc, 3 dc in last sc: 27 dc.

Note: Mark Row 2 as **right** side.

Row 3 (Increase row)**:** Ch 1, turn; working in Front Loops Only, 2 sc in first dc, sc in each dc across: 28 sc.

Rows 4-15: Repeat Rows 2 and 3, 6 times: 46 sc.

Row 16 (Increase row)**:** Ch 3, turn; working in Back Loops Only, dc in next sc and in each sc across to last sc, 3 dc in last sc: 48 dc.

Row 17 (Increase row)**:** Ch 1, turn; working in Front Loops Only, 3 sc in first dc, sc in each dc across: 50 sc.

Rows 18-31: Repeat Rows 16 and 17, 7 times: 78 sc.

Row 32: Ch 3, turn; dc in Back Loop Only of next sc and each sc across.

SHOULDER

Row 1: Ch {16-16-19}{19-21-21}, turn; sc in second ch from hook and in each ch across; sc in Front Loop Only of each dc across: {93-93-96}{96-98-98} sc.

Row 2: Ch 3, turn; dc in Back Loop Only of next sc and each sc across.

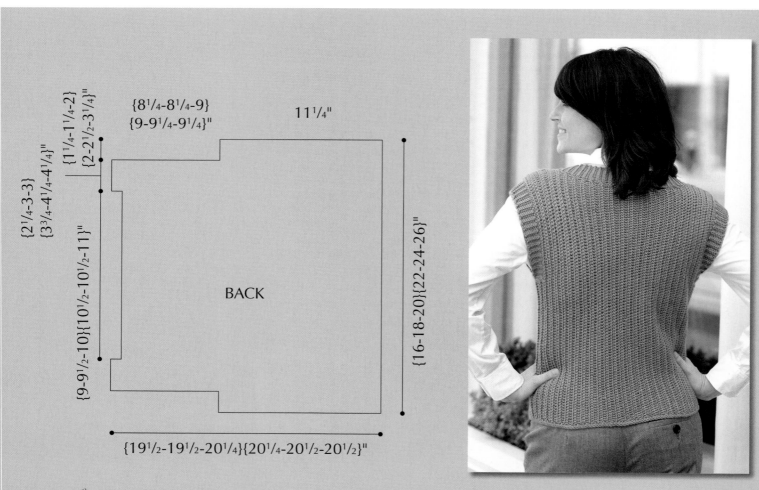

Row 3: Ch 1, turn; sc in Front Loop Only of each dc across.

Repeat Rows 2 and 3, {2-3-3}{4-5-5} times.

ARMHOLE
Row 1: Ch 3, turn; dc in Back Loop Only of next 53 sc, leave remaining sts unworked: 54 dc.

Row 2: Ch 1, turn; sc in Front Loop Only of each dc across.

Row 3: Ch 3, turn; dc in Back Loop Only of next sc and each sc across.

Row 4: Ch 1, turn; sc in Front Loop Only of each dc across.

Repeat Rows 3 and 4, {0-0-1}{1-2-3} time(s).

Finish off.

RIGHT FRONT
Right Front is worked from side-to-side, beginning at front edge.

With larger size hook, ch 26.

Row 1: Sc in second ch from hook and in each ch across: 25 sc.

Row 2 (Right side - Increase row)**:** Ch 3, turn; working in Back Loops Only, 3 dc in next sc, dc in next sc and in each sc across: 27 dc.

Note: Mark Row 2 as **right** side.

Row 3 (Increase row)**:** Ch 1, turn; working in Front Loops Only, sc in each dc across to last dc, 2 sc in last dc: 28 sc.

Rows 4-15: Repeat Rows 2 and 3, 6 times: 46 sc.

Instructions continued on page 40.

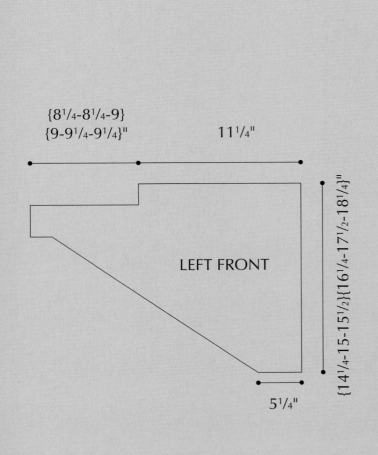

{8¹/₄-8¹/₄-9}
{9-9¹/₄-9¹/₄}"   11¹/₄"

LEFT FRONT

5¹/₄"

{14¹/₄-15-15¹/₂}{16¹/₄-17¹/₂-18¹/₄}"

Row 16 (Increase row)**:** Ch 3, turn; working in Back Loops Only, 3 dc in next sc, dc in next sc and in each sc across: 48 dc.

Row 17 (Increase row)**:** Ch 1, turn; working in Front Loops Only, sc in each dc across to last dc, 3 sc in last dc: 50 sc.

Rows 18-31: Repeat Rows 16 and 17, 7 times: 78 sc.

Finish off.

Place a marker at the increase end of Row {20-19-18}{17-18-17} for buttonhole placement.

Row 32: Ch {15-15-18}{18-20-20}; with **right** side facing, dc in Back Loop Only of each sc across Row 31.

SHOULDER
Row 1: Ch 1, turn; sc in Front Loop Only of each dc across, sc in each ch across: {93-93-96}{96-98-98} sc.

Row 2: Ch 3, turn; dc in Back Loop Only of next sc and each sc across.

Row 3: Ch 1, turn; sc in Front Loop Only of each dc across.

Repeat Rows 2 and 3, {2-3-3}{4-5-5} times.

Finish off.

ARMHOLE
Row 1: With **right** side facing, skip first {39-39-42}{42-44-44} sc and join yarn with slip st in Back Loop Only of next sc; ch 3, dc in Back Loop Only of next sc and each sc across: 54 dc.

Row 2: Ch 1, turn; sc in Front Loop Only of each dc across.

Row 3: Ch 3, turn; dc in Back Loop Only of next sc and each sc across.

Row 4: Ch 1, turn; sc in Front Loop Only of each dc across.

Repeat Rows 3 and 4, {0-0-1}{1-2-3} time(s).

Finish off.

FINISHING
Weave shoulder seams **(Fig. 6, page 127)**.

LEFT FRONT RIBBING
With smaller size hook, ch 11.

Row 1: Sc in second ch from hook and in each ch across: 10 sc.

Row 2: Ch 1, turn; sc in Back Loop Only of each sc across.

Repeat Row 2 until piece measures {2-2-2$\frac{1}{2}$}{2$\frac{3}{4}$-3-3$\frac{1}{4}$}"/{5-5-6.5}{7-7.5-8.5} cm less than measurement from lower edge to center of Back neck.

Finish off.

RIGHT FRONT RIBBING
With smaller size hook, ch 11.

Row 1: Sc in second ch from hook and in each ch across: 10 sc.

Rows 2-6: Ch 1, turn; sc in Back Loop Only of each sc across.

Row 7 (Buttonhole row)**:** Ch 1, turn; working in Back Loops Only, sc in first 4 sc, ch 2, skip next 2 sc (buttonhole made), sc in last 4 sc: 8 sc and one ch-2 sp.

Row 8: Ch 1, turn; working in Back Loops Only, sc in first 4 sc, 2 sc in next ch-2 sp, sc in last 4 sc: 10 sc.

Rows 9-18: Ch 1, turn; sc in Back Loop Only of each sc across.

Rows 19-68: Repeat Rows 7-18, 4 times; then repeat Rows 7 and 8 once **more**.

Complete same as Left Front Ribbing.

With **right** sides together, sew last row of Left and Right Front Ribbings together and pin seam to center of Back neck edge. Pin Ribbings to Left and Right Fronts, easing to fit, and matching top buttonhole to marked row on Right Front; then sew Ribbing in place.

ARMHOLE RIBBING (Make 2)
With smaller size hook, ch {9-9-9}{10-10-11}.

Row 1: Sc in second ch from hook and in each ch across: {8-8-8}{9-9-10} sc.

Row 2: Ch 1, turn; sc in Back Loop Only of each sc across.

Repeat Row 2 until piece measures approximately {15½-15½-17}{17-17½-17½}"/ {39.5-39.5-43}{43-44.5-44.5} cm from beginning ch.

Finish off.

Pin Armhole Ribbing to Armhole, matching sts on first and last row of ribbing to end of rows on armhole and easing end of rows on ribbing to fit armhole; then sew in place.

Whipstitch side seams **(Fig. 7, page 127)**.

BOTTOM EDGING
Row 1: With **right** side facing and using smaller size hook, join yarn with slip st in first ch of Left Front Ribbing; sc in each ch across Ribbing; working in end of rows across Left Front, Back, and Right Front, sc in next sc row, (2 sc in next dc row, sc in next sc row) across to Right Front Ribbing, sc in each ch across.

Row 2: Ch 1, turn; slip st in Front Loop Only of each sc across; finish off.

Lay piece flat with Right Front overlapping Left Front so combined Fronts measure same width as Back; then sew buttons to Left Front opposite buttonholes.

Classical Jacket

◼◼◼▭ **INTERMEDIATE**

Size	Finished Chest Measurement	
Extra Small	30"	(76 cm)
Small	34"	(86.5 cm)
Medium	38½"	(98 cm)
Large	42½"	(108 cm)
Extra Large	47"	(119.5 cm)
2X-Large	51"	(129.5 cm)
3X-Large	55½"	(141 cm)

Size Note: Instructions are written for size Extra Small with sizes Small, Medium, and Large in first set of braces { } and sizes Extra Large, 2X-Large, and 3X-Large in second set of braces. Instructions will be easier to read if you circle all the numbers pertaining to your size. If only one number is given, it applies to all sizes.

MATERIALS

Medium Weight Yarn
   [3.5 ounces, 220 yards
   (100 grams, 201 meters) per hank]:
      8{8-9-9}{10-10-11} hanks
Crochet hooks, sizes H (5 mm) **and** I (5.5 mm)
   or sizes needed for gauge
Yarn needle
Sewing needle and thread
⁷/₈" (22 mm) Buttons - 6

GAUGE: With smaller size hook,
            in peplum pattern,
            15 sts and 16 rows = 4" (10 cm)

Gauge Swatch: 4" (10 cm) square
With smaller size hook, ch 16.
Row 1: Sc in second ch from hook and in each ch across: 15 sc.
Row 2: Ch 1, turn; sc in first st, (dc in next st, sc in next st) across.
Row 3: Ch 3 **(counts as first dc)**, turn; (sc in next dc, dc in next sc) across.
Rows 4-16: Repeat Rows 2 and 3, 6 times; then repeat Row 2 once **more**.
Finish off.

Instructions continued on page 44.

STITCH GUIDE

RIGHT PLEAT (uses next 9 sts)
Insert hook in next st from the **front**, skip next 4 sts, insert hook in next st from the **back**, insert hook in next st from the **front**, YO and pull loop through all 3 sts, YO and draw through both loops on hook (**first sc made**), insert hook through first skipped st from the **front**, through fourth skipped st from the **back**, then through next unworked st from the **front**, YO and pull loop through all 3 sts, YO and draw through both loops on hook (**second sc made**); insert hook in second skipped sc from the **front**, through third skipped st from the **back**, then through next st from the **front**, YO and pull loop through all 3 sts, YO and draw through both loops on hook (**third sc made**).

LEFT PLEAT (uses next 9 sc)
Skip next 6 sts, insert hook in next st from the **front**, then through sixth skipped st from the **back**, then through first skipped st from the **front**, YO and pull loop through all 3 sts, YO and draw through both loops on hook (**first sc made**); insert hook in next unworked st from the **front**, through fifth skipped st from the **back**, then through second skipped st from the **front**, YO and pull loop through all 3 sts, YO and draw through both loops on hook (**second sc made**), insert hook in next st from the **front**, through fourth skipped st from the **back**, then through third skipped st from the **front**, YO and pull loop through all sts, YO and draw through both loops on hook (**third sc made**).

DECREASE
Pull up a loop in each of next 2 sts, YO and draw through all 3 loops on hook (**counts as one sc**).

BACK
PEPLUM

With smaller size hook, ch 93{101-109-117}{125-133-141}.

Row 1: Sc in second ch from hook and in each ch across: 92{100-108-116}{124-132-140} sc.

Row 2 (Right side)**:** Ch 1, turn; sc in first st, dc in next st, (sc in next st, dc in next st) across.

Note: Loop a short piece of yarn around any stitch to mark Row 2 as **right** side.

Repeat Row 2 for pattern until Back measures approximately 7½" (19 cm) from beginning ch, ending by working a **wrong** side row.

Pleat Row: Ch 1, turn; sc in first 6{7-8-10}{11-13-14} sts, work Right Pleat, [sc in next 5{6-7-8}{9-10-11} sts, work Right Pleat] twice, sc in next 6{8-10-10}{12-12-14} sts, work Left Pleat, [sc in next 5{6-7-8}{9-10-11} sts, work Left Pleat] twice, sc in last 6{7-8-10}{11-13-14} sts: 56{64-72-80}{88-96-104} sc.

Next Row: Ch 1, turn; sc in each sc across; do **not** finish off.

WAISTBAND
Change to larger size hook.

Row 1: Ch 1, turn; sc in first sc, ch 1, ★ skip next sc, sc in next sc, ch 1; repeat from ★ across to last 3 sc, skip next sc, sc in last 2 sc.

Rows 2-14: Ch 1, turn; sc in first sc, ★ ch 1, skip next sc, sc in next ch-1 sp; repeat from ★ across to last sc, sc in last sc; do **not** finish off.

BODY
Change to smaller size hook.

Row 1: Ch 1, turn; sc in first sc, dc in next sc, ★ sc in next ch-1 sp, dc in next sc; repeat from ★ across: 56{64-72-80}{88-96-104} sts.

Row 2: Ch 1, turn; sc in first dc, dc in next sc, (sc in next dc, dc in next sc) across.

Repeat Row 2 for pattern until Back measures approximately 15" (38 cm) from beginning ch, ending by working a **wrong** side row.

ARMHOLE SHAPING
Row 1: Turn; slip st in first 3{5-7-7}{9-11-13} sts, ch 1, sc in same st, dc in next sc, (sc in next dc, dc in next sc) across to last 2{4-6-6}{8-10-12} sts, leave remaining sts unworked: 52{56-60-68}{72-76-80} sts.

Row 2: Turn; slip st in first 3{5-5-7}{9-9-11} sts, ch 1, sc in same st, dc in next sc, (sc in next dc, dc in next sc) across to last 2{4-4-6}{8-8-10} sts, leave remaining sts unworked: 48{48-52-56}{56-60-60} sts.

Row 3: Ch 1, turn; sc in first dc, dc in next sc, (sc in next dc, dc in next sc) across.

Repeat Row 3 for pattern until Armholes measure approximately 8$\frac{1}{2}${8$\frac{1}{2}$-8$\frac{3}{4}$-8$\frac{3}{4}$}{9-9-9$\frac{1}{4}$}"/ 21.5{21.5-22-22}{23-23-23.5} cm, ending by working a **wrong** side row.

Instructions continued on page 46.

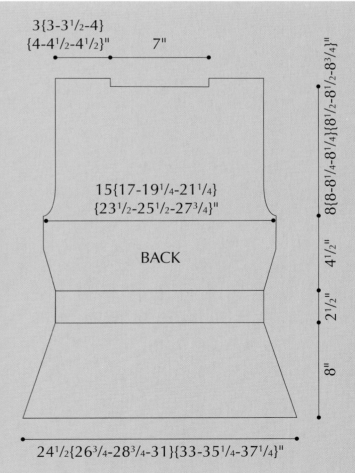

3{3-3$\frac{1}{2}$-4}{4-4$\frac{1}{2}$-4$\frac{1}{2}$}" 7"

15{17-19$\frac{1}{4}$-21$\frac{1}{4}$}{23$\frac{1}{2}$-25$\frac{1}{2}$-27$\frac{3}{4}$}"

BACK

8{8-8$\frac{1}{4}$-8$\frac{1}{4}$}{8$\frac{1}{2}$-8$\frac{1}{2}$-8$\frac{3}{4}$}"

4$\frac{1}{2}$"

2$\frac{1}{2}$"

8"

24$\frac{1}{2}${26$\frac{3}{4}$-28$\frac{3}{4}$-31}{33-35$\frac{1}{4}$-37$\frac{1}{4}$}"

RIGHT SHOULDER SHAPING

Row 1: Ch 1, turn; sc in first dc, (dc in next sc, sc in next dc) 5{5-6-7}{7-8-8} times, leave remaining sts unworked: 11{11-13-15}{15-17-17} sts.

Row 2: Ch 3 **(counts as first dc, now and throughout)**, turn; (sc in next dc, dc in next sc) across; finish off.

LEFT SHOULDER SHAPING

Row 1: With **right** side facing, skip next 26 sts from Right Shoulder Shaping and join yarn with slip st in next st; ch 3, (sc in next dc, dc in next sc) across: 11{11-13-15}{15-17-17} sts.

Row 2: Ch 1, turn; sc in first dc, (dc in next sc, sc in next dc) across; finish off.

LEFT FRONT

With smaller size hook, ch 59{63-67-71}{75-79-83}.

Row 1: Sc in second ch from hook and in each ch across: 58{62-66-70}{74-78-82} sc.

Row 2 (Right side): Ch 1, turn; sc in first st, dc in next st, (sc in next st, dc in next st) across.

Note: Mark Row 2 as **right** side.

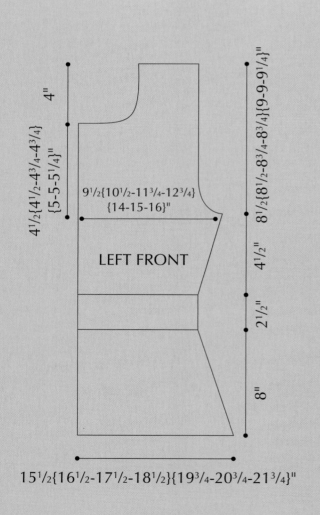

4"

$4^{1}/_{2}${$4^{1}/_{2}$-$4^{3}/_{4}$-$4^{3}/_{4}$}{5-5-$5^{1}/_{4}$}"

$9^{1}/_{2}${$10^{1}/_{2}$-$11^{3}/_{4}$-$12^{3}/_{4}$}{14-15-16}"

LEFT FRONT

$8^{1}/_{2}${$8^{1}/_{2}$-$8^{3}/_{4}$-$8^{3}/_{4}$}{9-9-$9^{1}/_{4}$}"

$4^{1}/_{2}$"

$2^{1}/_{2}$"

8"

$15^{1}/_{2}${$16^{1}/_{2}$-$17^{1}/_{2}$-$18^{1}/_{2}$}{$19^{3}/_{4}$-$20^{3}/_{4}$-$21^{3}/_{4}$}"

Repeat Row 2 for pattern until Left Front measures approximately 7½" (19 cm) from beginning ch, ending by working a **wrong** side row.

Pleat Row: Ch 1, turn; sc in first 4{4-6-8} {8-10-10} sts, decrease, work Right Pleat, ★ sc in next 2{2-3-3}{4-4-5} sts, decrease, sc in next 2{3-3-3}{4-4-5} sts, work Right Pleat; repeat from ★ once **more**, decrease, sc in last 11{13-13-15} {15-17-17} sts: 36{40-44-48}{52-56-60} sc.

Next Row: Ch 1, turn; sc in first 3{5-4-3} {5-5-4} sc, 2 sc in next sc, ★ sc in next 5{5-6-7} {7-8-9} sc, 2 sc in next sc; repeat from ★ across to last 2{4-4-4}{6-5-5} sc, sc in last 2{4-4-4} {6-5-5} sc: 42{46-50-54}{58-62-66} sc; do **not** finish off.

WAISTBAND
Change to larger size hook.

Row 1: Ch 1, turn; sc in first sc, ch 1, ★ skip next sc, sc in next sc, ch 1; repeat from ★ across to last 3 sc, skip next sc, sc in last 2 sc.

Rows 2-12: Ch 1, turn; sc in first sc, ★ ch 1, skip next sc, sc in next ch-1 sp; repeat from ★ across to last sc, sc in last sc.

Row 13: Ch 1, turn; sc in each sc and in each ch-1 sp across: 42{46-50-54}{58-62-66} sts.

Row 14: Ch 1, turn; sc in first 3{5-4-3}{5-5-4} sc, decrease, ★ sc in next 5{5-6-7}{7-8-9} sc, decrease; repeat from ★ across to last 2{4-4-4}{6-5-5} sc, sc in last 2{4-4-4}{6-5-5} sc; do **not** finish off: 36{40-44-48}{52-56-60} sc.

BODY
Change to smaller size hook.

Row 1: Ch 1, turn; sc in first sc, dc in next sc, (sc in next sc, dc in next sc) across.

Row 2: Ch 1, turn; sc in first dc, dc in next sc, (sc in next dc, dc in next sc) across.

Repeat Row 2 for pattern until Left Front measures same as Back to Armhole Shaping, ending by working a **wrong** side row.

ARMHOLE SHAPING
Row 1: Turn; slip st in first 3{5-7-7}{9-11-13} sts, ch 1, sc in same dc, dc in next sc, (sc in next dc, dc in next sc) across: 34{36-38-42}{44-46-48} sts.

Row 2: Ch 1, turn; sc in first dc, dc in next sc, (sc in next dc, dc in next sc) across to last 2{4-4-6}{8-8-10} sts, leave remaining sts unworked: 32{32-34-36}{36-38-38} sts.

Row 3: Ch 1, turn; sc in first dc, dc in next sc, (sc in next dc, dc in next sc) across.

Repeat Row 3 for pattern until Armhole measures approximately 4½{4½-4¾-4¾}{5-5-5¼}"/ 11.5{11.5-12-12}{12.5-12.5-13.5} cm, ending by working a **wrong** side row.

NECK SHAPING
Row 1: Ch 1, turn; sc in first dc, (dc in next sc, sc in next dc) across to last 7 sts, leave remaining sts unworked: 25{25-27-29}{29-31-31} sts.

Row 2 (Decrease row)**:** Turn; slip st in first 3 sts, ch 3, (sc in next dc, dc in next sc) across: 23{23-25-27}{27-29-29} sts.

Row 3 (Decrease row)**:** Ch 1, turn; sc in first dc, (dc in next sc, sc in next dc) across to last 2 sts, leave remaining sts unworked: 21{21-23-25} {25-27-27} sts.

Rows 4-8: Repeat Rows 2 and 3 twice, then repeat Row 2 once **more**: 11{11-13-15}{15-17-17} sts.

Instructions continued on page 48.

Row 9: Ch 1, turn; sc in first dc, (dc in next sc, sc in next dc) across.

Row 10: Ch 3, turn; (sc in next dc, dc in next sc) across.

Repeat Rows 9 and 10 until Left Front measures same as Back, ending by working a **wrong** side row.

Finish off.

Place markers for 3 buttons along Left Front center edge as follows: Place first marker at center of Waistband 2" (5 cm) from edge, place second marker ¹/₂" (1.5 cm) below neck edge, then place third marker between them so that the distance between the markers is equal.

RIGHT FRONT
Work same as Left Front to Pleat Row: 58{62-66-70}{74-78-82} sc.

Pleat Row: Ch 1, turn; sc in first 11{13-13-15}{15-17-17} sts, decrease, work Left Pleat, ★ sc in next 2{3-3-3}{4-4-5} sts, decrease, sc in next 2{2-3-3}{4-4-5} sts, work Left Pleat; repeat from ★ once **more**, decrease, sc in last 4{4-6-8}{8-10-10} sts: 36{40-44-48}{52-56-60} sc.

Next Row: Ch 1, turn; sc in first 2{4-4-4}{6-5-5} sc, 2 sc in next sc, ★ sc in next 5{5-6-7}{7-8-9} sc, 2 sc in next sc; repeat from ★ across to last 3{5-4-3}{5-5-4} sc, sc in last 3{5-4-3}{5-5-4} sc: 42{46-50-54}{58-62-66} sc.

WAISTBAND
Change to larger size hook.

Row 1: Ch 1, turn; sc in first sc, ch 1, ★ skip next sc, sc in next sc, ch 1; repeat from ★ across to last 3 sc, skip next sc, sc in last 2 sc.

Rows 2-6: Ch 1, turn; sc in first sc, ★ ch 1, skip next sc, sc in next ch-1 sp; repeat from ★ across to last sc, sc in last sc.

Row 7 (Buttonhole row)**:** Ch 1, turn; sc in first sc, (ch 1, skip next sc, sc in next ch-1 sp) twice, ch 3, skip next ch-1 sp, sc in next ch-1 sp (buttonhole made), ★ ch 1, skip next sc, sc in next ch-1 sp; repeat from ★ across to last sc, sc in last sc.

Row 8: Ch 1, turn; sc in first sc, ★ ch 1, skip next sc, sc in next ch-1 sp; repeat from ★ across to next ch-3 sp, (ch 1, sc) twice in ch-3 sp, (ch 1, skip next sc, sc in next ch-1 sp) twice, sc in last sc.

Rows 9-12: Ch 1, turn; sc in first sc, ★ ch 1, skip next sc, sc in next ch-1 sp; repeat from ★ across to last sc, sc in last sc.

Row 13: Ch 1, turn; sc in each sc and in each ch-1 sp across: 42{46-50-54}{58-62-66} sc.

Row 14: Ch 1, turn; sc in first 2{4-4-4}{6-5-5} sc, decrease, ★ sc in next 5{5-6-7}{7-8-9} sc, decrease; repeat from ★ across to last 3{5-4-3}{5-5-4} sc, sc in last 3{5-4-3}{5-5-4} sc; do **not** finish off: 36{40-44-48}{52-56-60} sc.

BODY
Work same as Left Front to next button marker, ending by working a **wrong** side row.

Buttonhole Row: Ch 1, turn; sc in first dc, (dc in next sc, sc in next dc) twice, ch 3, skip next 3 sts, sc in next dc (buttonhole made), dc in next sc, (sc in next dc, dc in next sc) across: 33{37-41-45}{49-53-57} sts and one ch-3 sp.

Next Row: Ch 1, turn; sc in first dc, dc in next sc, (sc in next dc, dc in next sc) across to ch-3 sp, (sc, dc, sc) in ch-3 sp, dc in next sc, (sc in next dc, dc in next sc) twice: 36{40-44-48}{52-56-60} sts.

Next Row: Ch 1, turn; sc in first dc, dc in next sc, (sc in next dc, dc in next sc) across.

Repeat last row until Right Front measures same as Back to Armhole Shaping, ending by working a **wrong** side row.

ARMHOLE SHAPING

Row 1: Ch 1, turn; sc in first dc, dc in next sc, (sc in next dc, dc in next sc) across to last 2{4-6-6}{8-10-12} sts, leave remaining sts unworked: 34{36-38-42}{44-46-48} sts.

Row 2: Turn; slip st in first 3{5-5-7}{9-9-11} sts, ch 1, sc in same st, dc in next sc, (sc in next dc, dc in next sc) across: 32{32-34-36}{36-38-38} sts.

Row 3: Ch 1, turn; sc in first dc, dc in next sc, (sc in next dc, dc in next sc) across.

Repeat Row 3 until Armhole measures same as Left Front to last button marker, ending by working a **wrong** side row.

Buttonhole Row: Ch 1, turn; sc in first dc, (dc in next sc, sc in next dc) twice, ch 3, skip next 3 sts, sc in next dc (buttonhole made), dc in next sc, (sc in next dc, dc in next sc) across: 29{29-31-33}{33-35-35} sts and one ch-3 sp.

Next Row: Ch 1, turn; sc in first dc, dc in next sc, (sc in next dc, dc in next sc) across to ch-3 sp, (sc, dc, sc) in ch-3 sp, dc in next sc, (sc in next dc, dc in next sc) twice: 32{32-34-36}{36-38-38} sts.

NECK SHAPING

Row 1: Turn; slip st in first 8 sts, ch 3, (sc in next dc, dc in next sc) across: 25{25-27-29}{29-31-31} sts.

Row 2: Ch 1, turn; sc in first dc, (dc in next sc, sc in next dc) across to last 2 sts, leave remaining sts unworked: 23{23-25-27}{27-29-29} sts.

Row 3: Turn; slip st in first 3 sts, ch 3, (sc in next dc, dc in next sc) across: 21{21-23-25}{25-27-27} sts.

Rows 4-8: Repeat Rows 2 and 3 twice, then repeat Row 2 once **more**: 11{11-13-15}{15-17-17} sts.

Row 9: Ch 3, turn; (sc in next dc, dc in next sc) across.

Row 10: Ch 1, turn; sc in first dc, (dc in next sc, sc in next dc) across.

Repeat Rows 9 and 10 until Right Front measures same as Left Front, ending by working a **wrong** side row.

Finish off.

RIGHT SLEEVE
PEPLUM
With smaller size hook, ch 63{67-71-75}{79-83-87}.

Row 1 (Right side)**:** Sc in second ch from hook and in each ch across: 62{66-70-74}{78-82-86} sc.

Note: Mark Row 1 as **right** side.

Row 2: Ch 1, turn; sc in first st, dc in next st, (sc in next st, dc in next st) across.

Repeat Row 2 until Right Sleeve measures approximately 4¹/₂" (11.5 cm) from beginning ch, ending by working a **wrong** side row.

Instructions continued on page 50.

Pleat Row: Ch 1, turn; sc in first 11{11-13-13}{13-15-15} sts, work Right Pleat, ★ sc in next 7{9-9-11}{13-13-15} sts, work Right Pleat; repeat from ★ once **more**, sc in last 10{10-12-12}{12-14-14} sts: 44{48-52-56}{60-64-68} sc.

Next Row: Ch 1, turn; sc in each sc across increasing 6 sts evenly spaced: 50{54-58-62}{66-70-74} sc.

SLEEVE BAND
Change to larger size hook.

Row 1: Ch 1, turn; sc in first sc, ch 1, ★ skip next sc, sc in next sc, ch 1; repeat from ★ across to last 3 sc, skip next sc, sc in last 2 sc: 26{28-30-32}{34-36-38} sts and 24{26-28-30}{32-34-36} ch-1 sps.

Rows 2-12: Ch 1, turn; sc in first sc, ★ ch 1, skip next sc, sc in next ch-1 sp; repeat from ★ across to last sc, sc in last sc.

Row 13: Ch 1, turn; sc in each sc and in each ch-1 sp across: 50{54-58-62}{66-70-74} sc.

Row 14: Ch 1, turn; sc in each sc across decreasing 6 sc evenly spaced: 44{48-52-56}{60-64-68} sc.

BODY
Change to smaller size hook.

Row 1: Ch 1, turn; sc in first st, dc in next st, (sc in next st, dc in next st) across.

Repeat Row 1 until Sleeve measures approximately 10½" (26.5 cm) from beginning ch, ending by working a **wrong** side row.

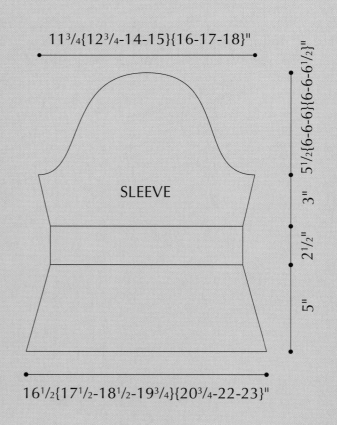

11¾{12¾-14-15}{16-17-18}"

5½{6-6-6}{6-6-6½}"

3"

2½"

5"

SLEEVE

16½{17½-18½-19¾}{20¾-22-23}"

CAP SHAPING

Row 1: Turn; slip st in first 3{5-7-7}{9-11-13} sts, ch 1, sc in same st, dc in next sc, (sc in next dc, dc in next sc) across to last 2{4-6-6}{8-10-12} sts, leave remaining sts unworked: 40{40-40-44}{44-44-44} sts.

Row 2: Turn; slip st in first 3{5-5-7}{9-9-11} sts, ch 1, sc in same st, dc in next sc, (sc in next dc, dc in next sc) across to last 2{4-4-6}{8-8-10} sts, leave remaining sts unworked: 36{32-32-32}{28-28-24} sts.

Size Extra Small ONLY

Row 3: Ch 1, turn; sc in first dc, dc in next sc, (sc in next dc, dc in next sc) across.

Row 4 (Decrease row)**:** Turn; slip st in first 2 sts, ch 3, sc in next dc, (dc in next sc, sc in next dc) across to last sc, leave last sc unworked: 34 sts.

Row 5: Ch 3, turn; sc in next dc, (dc in next sc, sc in next dc) across.

Row 6 (Decrease row)**:** Turn; slip st in first 2 sts, ch 1, sc in same st, dc in next sc, (sc in next dc, dc in next sc) across to last dc, leave last dc unworked: 32 sts.

Rows 7-22: Repeat Rows 3-6, 4 times: 16 sts.

Finish off.

Sizes Small, Medium, & Large ONLY

Row 3: Ch 1, turn; sc in first dc, dc in next sc, (sc in next dc, dc in next sc) across.

Row 4 (Decrease row)**:** Turn; slip st in first 2 sts, ch 3, sc in next dc, (dc in next sc, sc in next dc) across to last sc, leave last sc unworked: 30 sts.

Row 5: Ch 3, turn; sc in next dc, (dc in next sc, sc in next dc) across.

Row 6 (Decrease row)**:** Turn; slip st in first 2 sts, ch 1, sc in same st, dc in next sc, (sc in next dc, dc in next sc) across to last dc, leave last dc unworked: 28 sts.

Rows 7-12: Repeat Rows 3-6 once, then repeat Rows 3 and 4 once **more**: 22 sts.

Rows 13-15: Ch 3, turn; sc in next dc, (dc in next sc, sc in next dc) across.

Row 16 (Decrease row)**:** Turn; slip st in first 2 sts, ch 1, sc in same dc, dc in next sc, (sc in next dc, dc in next sc) across to last dc, leave last dc unworked: 20 sts.

Rows 17-19: Ch 1, turn; sc in first dc, dc in next sc, (sc in next dc, dc in next sc) across.

Row 20 (Decrease row)**:** Turn; slip st in first 2 sts, ch 3, sc in next dc, (dc in next sc, sc in next dc) across to last sc, leave last sc unworked: 18 sts.

Rows 21-24: Repeat Rows 13-16: 16 sts.

Finish off.

Instructions continued on page 52.

Sizes Extra Large & 2X-Large ONLY
Row 3: Ch 1, turn; sc in first dc, dc in next sc, (sc in next dc, dc in next sc) across.

Row 4 (Decrease row)**:** Turn; slip st in first 2 sts, ch 3, sc in next dc, (dc in next sc, sc in next dc) across to last sc, leave last sc unworked: 26 sts.

Rows 5-7: Ch 3, turn; sc in next dc, (dc in next sc, sc in next dc) across.

Row 8 (Decrease row)**:** Turn; slip st in first 2 sts, ch 1, sc in same dc, dc in next sc, (sc in next dc, dc in next sc) across to last dc, leave last dc unworked: 24 sts.

Rows 9-11: Ch 1, turn; sc in first dc, dc in next sc, (sc in next dc, dc in next sc) across.

Row 12 (Decrease row)**:** Turn; slip st in first 2 sts, ch 3, sc in next dc, (dc in next sc, sc in next dc) across to last sc, leave last sc unworked: 22 sts.

Rows 13-15: Ch 3, turn; sc in next dc, (dc in next sc, sc in next dc) across.

Rows 16-24: Repeat Rows 8-15 once, then repeat Row 8 once **more**: 16 sts.

Finish off.

Size 3X-Large ONLY
Rows 3-7: Ch 1, turn; sc in first dc, dc in next sc, (sc in next dc, dc in next sc) across.

Row 8 (Decrease row)**:** Turn; slip st in first 2 sts, ch 3, sc in next dc, ★ dc in next sc, sc in next dc; repeat from ★ across to last sc, leave last sc unworked: 22 sts.

Rows 9-13: Ch 3, turn; sc in next dc, (dc in next sc, sc in next dc) across.

Row 14 (Decrease row)**:** Turn; slip st in first 2 sts, ch 1, sc in same st, dc in next sc, ★ sc in next dc, dc in next sc; repeat from ★ across to last dc, leave last dc unworked: 20 sts.

Rows 15-26: Repeat Rows 3-14: 16 sts.

Finish off.

LEFT SLEEVE
PEPLUM
Work same as Right Sleeve to Pleat Row: 62{66-70-74}{78-82-86} sts.

Pleat Row: Ch 1, turn; sc in first 10{10-12-12}{12-14-14} sts, work Left Pleat, ★ sc in next 7{9-9-11}{13-13-15} sts, work Left Pleat; repeat from ★ once **more**; sc in last 11{11-13-13}{13-15-15} sts: 44{48-52-56}{60-64-68} sc.

Complete same as Right Sleeve.

COLLAR
With larger size hook, ch 89.

Row 1 (Right side)**:** Sc in second ch from hook and in each ch across: 88 sc.

Note: Mark Row 1 as **right** side.

Row 2: Ch 1, turn; sc in first sc, ch 1, ★ skip next sc, sc in next sc, ch 1; repeat from ★ across to last 3 sc, skip next sc, sc in last 2 sc.

Rows 3-16: Ch 1, turn; sc in first sc, ★ ch 1, skip next sc, sc in next ch-1 sp; repeat from ★ across to last sc, sc in last sc.

Finish off.

FINISHING

Whipstitch shoulder seams *(Fig. 7, page 127)*.

Weave Sleeves to Jacket *(Fig. 6, page 127)*.

Weave underarm and side in one continuous seam.

FRONT EDGING

With **right** side facing, using larger size hook, and working in end of rows, join yarn with slip st in bottom corner of Right Front; ch 1, sc in same st, sc evenly across Front to neck edge, 3 sc in corner, sc evenly around neck to left corner, 3 sc in corner, sc evenly across Left Front edge; finish off.

Sew beginning ch of Collar to neck edge, beginning and ending 3" (7.5 mm) from Front corners.

COLLAR EDGING

With **right** side facing and using larger size hook, and working in end of rows and across Row 16, join yarn with slip st in Collar at seam; ch 1, sc evenly around Collar working 3 sc in each corner; finish off.

Sew 3 buttons to Left Front opposite buttonholes; sew remaining 3 buttons to Right Front, each approximately 2" (5 cm) from buttonhole.

Blue Heaven Sweater

■■□□ EASY

Size	Finished Chest Measurement
Extra Small	31" (78.5 cm)
Small	35" (89 cm)
Medium	39" (99 cm)
Large	43" (109 cm)
Extra Large	47" (119.5 cm)
2X-Large	51" (129.5 cm)

Size Note: Instructions are written with sizes Extra Small, Small, and Medium in first set of braces { } and sizes Large, Extra Large, and 2X-Large in second set of braces. Instructions will be easier to read if you circle all the numbers pertaining to your size. If only one number is given, it applies to all sizes.

MATERIALS

Medium Weight Yarn
[3 ounces, 185 yards
(85 grams, 170 meters) per skein]:
{5-6-6}{7-7-8} skeins
Crochet hook, size I (5.5 mm) **or** size needed
for gauge
Yarn needle
Sewing needle and thread
⁷/₈" (22 mm) Button

GAUGE: In pattern, 4 repeats
and 8 rows = 4" (10 cm)

Gauge Swatch: 3¹/₂"w x 4"h (9 cm x 10 cm)
Ch 28.
Work same as Rows 1-8 of Back, page 56:
16 sts and 3 ch-3 sps.
Finish off.

Instructions continued on page 56.

BACK

Ch {112-126-140}{154-168-182}.

Row 1 (Right side)**:** 2 Dc in fourth ch from hook **(3 skipped chs count as first dc)**, skip next 2 chs, sc in next ch, ★ ch 3, dc in next 3 chs, skip next 3 chs, sc in next ch; repeat from ★ across: {64-72-80}{88-96-104} sts and {15-17-19}{21-23-25} ch-3 sps.

Note: Loop a short piece of yarn around any stitch to mark Row 1 as **right** side.

Row 2: Ch 3 **(counts as first dc, now and throughout)**, turn; 2 dc in first sc, skip next 2 dc, sc in next dc, ★ ch 3, dc in next 3 chs, skip next 3 sts, sc in next dc; repeat from ★ across.

Repeat Row 2 for pattern until Back measures approximately 10½" (26.5 cm) from beginning ch, ending by working a **wrong** side row.

ARMHOLE SHAPING

Row 1: Turn; slip st in first {3-3-3}{3-10-10} sts and chs, ch 1, sc in next dc, ★ ch 3, dc in next 3 chs, skip next 3 sts, sc in next dc; repeat from ★ {13-15-17}{19-19-21} times **more**, leave remaining sts unworked: {57-65-73}{81-81-89} sts and {14-16-18}{20-20-22} ch-3 sps.

Row 2: Ch 3, turn; 2 dc in first sc, skip next 2 dc, sc in next dc, ★ ch 3, dc in next 3 chs, skip next 3 sts, sc in next dc; repeat from ★ {12-14-16}{18-18-20} times **more**, leave remaining sts unworked: {56-64-72}{80-80-88} sts and {13-15-17}{19-19-21} ch-3 sps.

Sizes Extra Small and Small ONLY
Rows 3-14: Ch 3, turn; 2 dc in first sc, skip next 2 dc, sc in next dc, ★ ch 3, dc in next 3 chs, skip next 3 sts, sc in next dc; repeat from ★ across.

Finish off.

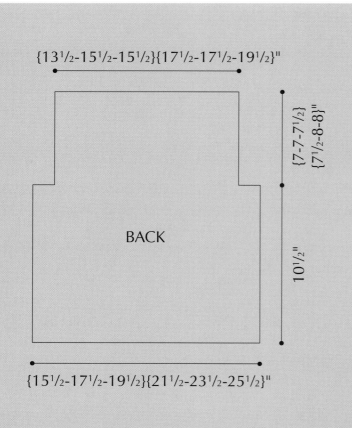

{13½-15½-15½}{17½-17½-19½}"

{7-7-7½}{7½-8-8}"

BACK

10½"

{15½-17½-19½}{21½-23½-25½}"

Sizes Medium, Large, Extra Large, & 2X-Large ONLY
Row 3: Turn; slip st in first 3 sts, ch 1, sc in next dc, ★ ch 3, dc in next 3 chs, skip next 3 sts, sc in next dc; repeat from ★ {15}{17-17-19} times **more**, leave remaining sts unworked: {65}{73-73-81} sts and {16}{18-18-20} ch-3 sps.

Row 4: Ch 3, turn; 2 dc in first sc, skip next 2 dc, sc in next dc, ★ ch 3, dc in next 3 chs, skip next 3 sts, sc in next dc; repeat from ★ {14}{16-16-18} times **more**, leave remaining sts unworked: {64}{72-72-80} sts and {15}{17-17-19} ch-3 sps.

Rows 5 thru {15}{15-16-16}: Ch 3, turn; 2 dc in first sc, skip next 2 dc, sc in next dc, ★ ch 3, dc in next 3 chs, skip next 3 sts, sc in next dc; repeat from ★ across.

Finish off.

RIGHT FRONT
Ch {56-63-70}{77-84-91}.

Work same as Back, page 56, to Armhole Shaping: {32-36-40}{44-48-52} sts and {7-8-9}{10-11-12} ch-3 sps.

ARMHOLE AND NECK SHAPING
Row 1: Turn; slip st in first 3 sts, ch 1, sc in next dc, ★ ch 3, dc in next 3 chs, skip next 3 sts, sc in next dc; repeat from ★ {5-6-7}{8-8-9} times **more**, leave remaining sts unworked: {25-29-33} {37-37-41} sts and {6-7-8}{9-9-10} ch-3 sps.

Row 2: Ch 3, turn; 2 dc in first sc, skip next 2 dc, sc in next dc, ★ ch 3, dc in next 3 chs, skip next 3 sts, sc in next dc; repeat from ★ {4-5-6}{7-7-8} times **more**, leave remaining sts unworked: {24-28-32}{36-36-40} sts and {5-6-7}{8-8-9} ch-3 sps.

Sizes Extra Small & Small ONLY
Rows 3 and 4: Ch 3, turn; 2 dc in first sc, skip next 2 dc, sc in next dc, ★ ch 3, dc in next 3 chs, skip next 3 sts, sc in next dc; repeat from ★ across.

Sizes Medium, Large, Extra Large, & 2X-Large ONLY
Row 3: Ch 3, turn; 2 dc in first sc, skip next 2 dc, sc in next dc, ★ ch 3, dc in next 3 chs, skip next 3 sts, sc in next dc; repeat from ★ {5}{6-6-7} times **more**, leave remaining sts unworked: {28}{32-32-36} sts and {6}{7-7-8} ch-3 sps.

Row 4: Ch 3, turn; 2 dc in first sc, skip next 2 dc, sc in next dc, ★ ch 3, dc in next 3 chs, skip next 3 sts, sc in next dc; repeat from ★ across.

All Sizes
Row 5: Turn; slip st in first 3 sts, ch 1, sc in next dc, ★ ch 3, dc in next 3 chs, skip next 3 sts, sc in next dc; repeat from ★ across: {21-25-25}{29-29-33} sts and {5-6-6}{7-7-8} ch-3 sps.

Row 6: Ch 3, turn; 2 dc in first sc, skip next 2 dc, sc in next dc, ★ ch 3, dc in next 3 chs, skip next 3 sts, sc in next dc; repeat from ★ across to last ch-3 sp and sc, leave last ch-3 and sc unworked: {20-24-24}{28-28-32} sts and {4-5-5}{6-6-7} ch-3 sps.

Rows 7 and 8: Ch 3, turn; 2 dc in first sc, skip next 2 dc, sc in next dc, ★ ch 3, dc in next 3 chs, skip next 3 sts, sc in next dc; repeat from ★ across.

Rows 9 thru {14-14-15}{15-16-16}: Repeat Rows 5-8 once, then repeat Rows 5 thru {6-6-7} {7-8-8} once **more**: {12-16-16}{20-20-24} sts and {2-3-3}{4-4-5} ch-3 sps.

Finish off.

LEFT FRONT
Ch {56-63-70}{77-84-91}.

Work same as Back, page 56, to Armhole Shaping: {32-36-40}{44-48-52} sts and {7-8-9}{10-11-12} ch-3 sps.

Instructions continued on page 58.

ARMHOLE AND NECK SHAPING

Row 1: Turn; slip st in first {3-3-3}{3-10-10} sts and chs, ch 1, sc in next dc, ★ ch 3, dc in next 3 chs, skip next 3 sts, sc in next dc; repeat from ★ {5-6-7}{8-8-9} times **more**, leave remaining sts unworked: {25-29-33}{37-37-41} sts and {6-7-8}{9-9-10} ch-3 sps.

Row 2: Ch 3, turn; 2 dc in first sc, skip next 2 dc, sc in next dc, ★ ch 3, dc in next 3 chs, skip next 3 sts, sc in next dc; repeat from ★ {4-5-6}{7-7-8} times **more**, leave remaining sts unworked: {24-28-32}{36-36-40} sts and {5-6-7}{8-8-9} ch-3 sps.

Sizes Extra Small & Small ONLY

Rows 3 and 4: Ch 3, turn; 2 dc in first sc, skip next 2 dc, sc in next dc, ★ ch 3, dc in next 3 chs, skip next 3 sts, sc in next dc; repeat from ★ across.

Sizes Medium, Large, Extra Large, & 2X-Large ONLY

Row 3: Turn; slip st in first 3 sts, ch 1, sc in next dc, ★ ch 3, dc in next 3 chs, skip next 3 sts, sc in next dc; repeat from ★ across: {29}{33-33-37} sts and {7}{8-8-9} ch-3 sps.

Row 4: Ch 3, turn; 2 dc in first sc, skip next 2 dc, sc in next dc, ★ ch 3, dc in next 3 chs, skip next 3 sts, sc in next dc; repeat from ★ {5}{6-6-7} times **more**, leave remaining sts unworked: {28}{32-32-36} sts and {6}{7-7-8} ch-3 sps.

All Sizes

Row 5: Ch 3, turn; 2 dc in first sc, skip next 2 dc, sc in next dc, ★ ch 3, dc in next 3 chs, skip next 3 sts, sc in next dc; repeat from ★ {3-4-4}{5-5-6} times **more**, leave remaining sts unworked: {20-24-24}{28-28-32} sts and {4-5-5}{6-6-7} ch-3 sps.

Rows 6-8: Ch 3, turn; 2 dc in first sc, skip next 2 dc, sc in next dc, ★ ch 3, dc in next 3 chs, skip next 3 sts, sc in next dc; repeat from ★ across.

Row 9: Ch 3, turn; 2 dc in first sc, skip next 2 dc, sc in next dc, ★ ch 3, dc in next 3 chs, skip next 3 sts, sc in next dc; repeat from ★ {2-3-3}{4-4-5} times **more**, leave remaining sts unworked: {16-20-20}{24-24-28} sts and {3-4-4}{5-5-6} ch-3 sps.

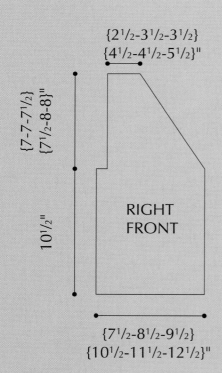

{2¹/₂-3¹/₂-3¹/₂}
{4¹/₂-4¹/₂-5¹/₂}"

{7-7-7¹/₂}
{7¹/₂-8-8}"

10¹/₂"

RIGHT FRONT

{7¹/₂-8¹/₂-9¹/₂}
{10¹/₂-11¹/₂-12¹/₂}"

Rows 10-12: Ch 3, turn; 2 dc in first sc, skip next 2 dc, sc in next dc, ★ ch 3, dc in next 3 chs, skip next 3 sts, sc in next dc; repeat from ★ across.

Row 13: Ch 3, turn; 2 dc in first sc, skip next 2 dc, sc in next dc, ★ ch 3, dc in next 3 chs, skip next 3 sts, sc in next dc; repeat from ★ {1-2-2}{3-3-4} time(s) **more**, leave remaining sts unworked: {12-16-16}{20-20-24} sts and {2-3-3}{4-4-5} ch-3 sps.

Last {1-1-2}{2-3-3} Rows: Ch 3, turn; 2 dc in first sc, skip next 2 dc, sc in next dc, ★ ch 3, dc in next 3 chs, skip next 3 sts, sc in next dc; repeat from ★ across.

Finish off.

SLEEVE (Make 2)
Ch {112-119-119}{126-126-133}.

Row 1 (Right side): 2 Dc in fourth ch from hook **(3 skipped chs count as first dc)**, skip next 2 chs, sc in next ch, ★ ch 3, dc in next 3 chs, skip next 3 chs, sc in last ch; repeat from ★ across: {64-68-68}{72-72-76} sts and {15-16-16}{17-17-18} ch-3 sps.

Note: Mark Row 1 as **right** side.

Rows 2 and 3: Ch 3, turn; 2 dc in first sc, skip next 2 dc, sc in next dc, ★ ch 3, dc in next 3 chs, skip next 3 sts, sc in next dc; repeat from ★ across.

Row 4: Turn; slip st in first 3 sts, ch 1, sc in next dc, ★ ch 3, dc in next 3 chs, skip next 3 sts, sc in next dc; repeat from ★ {13-14-14}{15-15-16} times **more**, leave remaining sts unworked: {57-61-61}{65-65-69} sts and {14-15-15}{16-16-17} ch-3 sps.

Row 5: Ch 3, turn; 2 dc in first sc, skip next 2 dc, sc in next dc, ★ ch 3, dc in next 3 chs, skip next 3 sts, sc in next dc; repeat from ★ across to last ch-3 and sc, leave remaining ch-3 and sc unworked: {56-60-60}{64-64-68} sts and {13-14-14}{15-15-16} ch-3 sps.

Row 6: Ch 3, turn; 2 dc in first sc, skip next 2 dc, sc in next dc, ★ ch 3, dc in next 3 chs, skip next 3 sts, sc in next dc; repeat from ★ across.

Row 7: Turn; slip st in first 3 sts, ch 1, sc in next dc, ★ ch 3, dc in next 3 chs, skip next 3 sts, sc in next dc; repeat from ★ {11-12-12}{13-13-14} times **more**, leave remaining sts unworked: {49-53-53}{57-57-61} sts and {12-13-13}{14-14-15} ch-3 sps.

Row 8: Repeat Row 5: {48-52-52}{56-56-60} sts and {11-12-12}{13-13-14} ch-3 sps.

Rows 9-16: Ch 3, turn; 2 dc in first sc, skip next 2 dc, sc in next dc, ★ ch 3, dc in next 3 chs, skip next 3 sts, sc in next dc; repeat from ★ across.

CAP SHAPING
Row 1: Turn; slip st in first 3 sts, ch 1, sc in next dc, ★ ch 3, dc in next 3 chs, skip next 3 sts, sc in next dc; repeat from ★ {9-10-10}{11-11-12} times **more**, leave remaining sts unworked: {41-45-45}{49-49-53} sts and {10-11-11}{12-12-13} ch-3 sps.

Row 2: Ch 3, turn; 2 dc in first sc, skip next 2 dc, sc in next dc, ★ ch 3, dc in next 3 chs, skip next 3 sts, sc in next dc; repeat from ★ across to last ch-3 and sc, leave remaining ch-3 and sc unworked: {40-44-44}{48-48-52} sts and {9-10-10}{11-11-12} ch-3 sps.

Row 3: Turn; slip st in first 3 sts, ch 1, sc in next dc, ★ ch 3, dc in next 3 chs, skip next 3 sts, sc in next dc; repeat from ★ {7-8-8}{9-9-10} times **more**, leave remaining sts unworked: {33-37-37}{41-41-45} sts and {8-9-9}{10-10-11} ch-3 sps.

Row 4: Repeat Row 2: {32-36-36}{40-40-44} sts and {7-8-8}{9-9-10} ch-3 sps.

Rows 5 and 6: Ch 3, turn; 2 dc in first sc, skip next 2 dc, sc in next dc, ★ ch 3, dc in next 3 chs, skip next 3 sts, sc in next dc; repeat from ★ across.

Instructions continued on page 60.

Row 7: Turn; slip st in first 3 sts, ch 1, sc in next dc, ★ ch 3, dc in next 3 chs, skip next 3 sts, sc in next dc; repeat from ★ {5-6-6}{7-7-8} times **more**, leave remaining sts unworked: {25-29-29} {33-33-37} sts and {6-7-7}{8-8-9} ch-3 sps.

Row 8: Repeat Row 2: {24-28-28}{32-32-36} sts and {5-6-6}{7-7-8} ch-3 sps.

Row 9: Turn; slip st in first 3 sts, ch 1, sc in next dc, ★ ch 3, dc in next 3 chs, skip next 3 sts, sc in next dc; repeat from ★ {3-4-4}{5-5-6} times **more**, leave remaining sts unworked: {17-21-21} {25-25-29} sts and {4-5-5}{6-6-7} ch-3 sps.

Row 10: Repeat Row 2: {16-20-20}{24-24-28} sts and {3-4-4}{5-5-6} ch-3 sps.

Row 11: Turn; slip st in first 3 sts, ch 1, sc in next dc, ★ ch 3, dc in next 3 chs, skip next 3 sts, sc in next dc; repeat from ★ {1-2-2}{3-3-4} time(s) **more**, leave remaining sts unworked; finish off: {9-13-13}{17-17-21} sts and {2-3-3}{4-4-5} ch-3 sps.

FINISHING

Whipstitch shoulder seams *(Fig. 7, page 127)*.

Weave Sleeves to Cardigan *(Fig. 6, page 127)*.

Weave underarm and side in one continuous seam.

BODY EDGING

Row 1: With **right** side facing, join yarn with slip st in bottom corner of Right Front; ch 1, work 34 sc evenly spaced across to beginning of Neck Shaping, sc evenly around remaining neck and center front edge to bottom corner of Left Front.

Row 2: Ch 1, turn; sc in each sc across.

Row 3: Ch 3 **(counts as first dc)**, turn; dc in next sc and in each sc across.

Row 4: Ch 1, turn; sc in each dc across.

Row 5 (Buttonhole row)**:** Ch 1, turn; sc in first 34 sc, ch 3, skip next 2 sc (buttonhole made), sc in each sc across; finish off.

Sew button to Left Front opposite buttonhole.

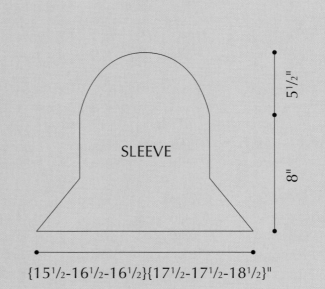

SLEEVE

5¹/₂"

8"

{15¹/₂-16¹/₂-16¹/₂}{17¹/₂-17¹/₂-18¹/₂}"

Something Special Cardigan

Shown on page 63.

 EASY

Size	Finished Chest Measurement
Extra Small	30" (76 cm)
Small	34^1/$_2$" (87.5 cm)
Medium	38^1/$_2$" (98 cm)
Large	42" (106.5 cm)
Extra Large	46" (117 cm)
2X-Large	50^1/$_2$" (128.5 cm)
3X-Large	54^1/$_2$" (138.5 cm)

Size Note: Instructions are written for size Extra Small with sizes Small, Medium, and Large in first set of braces { } and sizes Extra Large, 2X-Large, and 3X-Large in second set of braces. Instructions will be easier to read if you circle all the numbers pertaining to your size. If only one number is given, it applies to all sizes.

MATERIALS

Light Weight Yarn **3**
[3 ounces, 251 yards
(85 grams, 230 meters) per skein]:
5{6-6-7}{7-8-8} skeins
Crochet hook, size H (5 mm) **or** size needed
for gauge
Yarn needle
Sewing needle and thread
^{7}/$_8$" (22 mm) Button

GAUGE: 19 sc and 21 sc rows = 4" (10 cm)

Gauge Swatch: 4" (10 cm) square
Ch 20.
Row 1: Sc in second ch from hook and in each ch across: 19 sc.
Rows 2-21: Ch 1, turn; sc in each sc across.
Finish off.

Instructions continued on page 62.

STITCH GUIDE

BACK POST TREBLE CROCHET
(abbreviated BPtr)
YO twice, insert hook from **back** to **front** around post of st indicated *(Fig. 4, page 126)*, YO and pull up a loop (4 loops on hook), (YO and draw through 2 loops on hook) 3 times.

FRONT POST TREBLE CROCHET
(abbreviated FPtr)
YO twice, insert hook from **front** to **back** around post of st indicated *(Fig. 4, page 126)*, YO and pull up a loop (4 loops on hook), (YO and draw through 2 loops on hook) 3 times.

BACK

Ch 73{83-93-101}{111-121-131}.

Row 1 (Wrong side)**:** Sc in second ch from hook and in each ch across: 72{82-92-100}{110-120-130} sc.

Note: Loop a short piece of yarn around back of any stitch on Row 1 to mark **right** side.

Row 2: Ch 1, turn; sc in each sc across.

Repeat Row 2 until Back measures approximately 3½{3½-3¾-3¾}{4-4-4¼}"/9{9-9.5-9.5}{10-10-11} cm from beginning ch.

ARMHOLE SHAPING

Row 1: Turn; slip st in first 5{7-10-11}{14-16-18} sc, ch 1, sc in next sc and in each sc across to last 5{7-10-11}{14-16-18} sc, leave remaining sc unworked: 62{68-72-78}{82-88-94} sc.

Row 2: Ch 1, turn; sc in each sc across.

Repeat Row 2 until armholes measure approximately 7{7¼-7½-7¾}{8-8¼-8½}"/18{18.5-19-19.5}{20.5-21-21.5} cm.

Finish off.

Instructions continued on page 64.

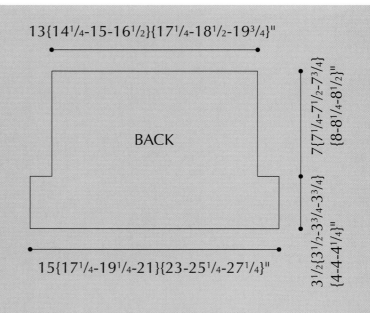

13{14¼-15-16½}{17¼-18½-19¾}"

BACK

7{7¼-7½-7¾}{8-8¼-8½}"

3½{3½-3¾-3¾}{4-4-4¼}"

15{17¼-19¼-21}{23-25¼-27¼}"

FRONT (Make 2)

Ch 37{42-47-51}{56-61-66}.

Row 1 (Wrong side)**:** Sc in second ch from hook and in each ch across: 36{41-46-50}{55-60-65} sc.

Note: Mark back of Row 1 as **right** side.

Rows 2-6: Ch 1, turn; sc in each sc across.

NECK AND ARMHOLE SHAPING

Row 1 (Decrease row)**:** Ch 1, turn; skip first sc, sc in next sc and in each sc across: 35{40-45-49}{54-59-64} sc.

Row 2: Ch 1, turn; sc in each sc across.

Rows 3-11: Repeat Rows 1 and 2, 4 times; then repeat Row 1 once **more**: 30{35-40-44}{49-54-59} sc.

When Front measures approximately 3½{3½-3¾-3¾}{4-4-4¼}"/9{9-9.5-9.5}{10-10-11} cm from beginning ch, work armhole shaping on right side row as follows: Turn; slip st in first 5{7-10-11}{14-16-18} sc, ch 1, sc in each sc across.

Rows 12-14: Ch 1, turn; sc in each sc across.

Rows 15-19: Repeat Rows 1 and 2 twice, then repeat Row 1 once **more**.

Rows 20-22: Ch 1, turn; sc in each sc across.

Repeat Rows 15-22 until there are 13{13-15-17}{19-21-23} sts remaining.

Work even until armhole measures same as Back.

Finish off leaving a long end for sewing.

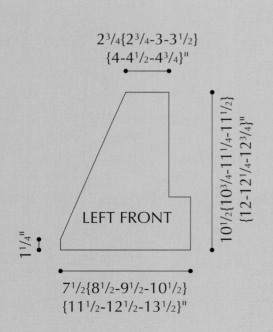

2³/₄{2³/₄-3-3½}
{4-4½-4³/₄}"

10½{10³/₄-11¼-11½}
{12-12¼-12³/₄}"

1¼"

LEFT FRONT

7½{8½-9½-10½}
{11½-12½-13½}"

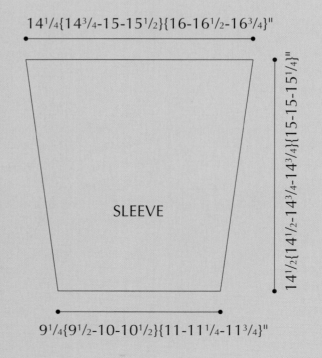

14¼{14³/₄-15-15½}{16-16½-16³/₄}"

14½{14½-14³/₄-14³/₄}{15-15-15¼}"

SLEEVE

9¼{9½-10-10½}{11-11¼-11³/₄}"

SLEEVE (Make 2)

Ch 45{47-49-51}{53-55-57}.

Row 1 (Wrong side)**:** Sc in second ch from hook and in each ch across: 44{46-48-50}{52-54-56} sc.

Note: Mark back of Row 1 as **right** side.

Row 2: Ch 1, turn; sc in each sc across.

Row 3 (Increase row)**:** Ch 1, 2 sc in first sc, sc in next sc and in each sc across to last sc, 2 sc in last sc: 46{48-50-52}{54-56-58} sc.

Rows 4-6: Ch 1, turn; sc in each sc across.

Rows 7-50: Repeat Rows 3-6, 11 times: 68{70-72-74}{76-78-80} sc.

Work even until Sleeve measures approximately 14½{14½-14¾-14¾}{15-15-15¼}"/ 37{37-37.5-37.5}{38-38-38.5} cm from beginning ch.

Finish off.

FINISHING

Whipstitch shoulder seams *(Fig. 7, page 127)*.

Weave Sleeves to Cardigan *(Fig. 6, page 127)*.

Weave underarm and side in one continuous seam.

PEPLUM

Row 1: With **right** side facing and working in free loops of beginning ch *(Fig. 2, page 126)*, join yarn with dc in first ch on Left Front *(see Joining With Dc, page 125)*; skip next ch, dc in next ch and in each ch across: 143{163-183-199}{219-239-259} dc.

Row 2: Ch 3 **(counts as first dc, now and throughout)**, turn; work BPtr around next dc, ★ dc in next dc, 2 dc in next dc, dc in next dc, work BPtr around next dc; repeat from ★ across to last dc, dc in last dc: 178{203-228-248}{273-298-323} sts.

Row 3: Ch 3, turn; work FPtr around next BPtr, ★ dc in next 4 dc, work FPtr around next BPtr; repeat from ★ across to last dc, dc in last dc.

Row 4: Ch 3, turn; work BPtr around next FPtr, ★ dc in next 4 dc, work BPtr around next FPtr; repeat from ★ across to last dc, dc in last dc.

Rows 5-15: Repeat Rows 3 and 4, 5 times; then repeat Row 3 once **more**; do **not** finish off.

BAND

Row 1: Ch 1, do **not** turn; working in end of rows across Peplum; 2 sc in each of first 15 rows; working across end of rows on Right Front, 2 sc in next row, ch 3, skip next row, sc in next row (button loop made), sc in each row across, sc in each st across Back neck edge, sc in each row across Left Front to Peplum, 2 sc in each of last 15 rows.

Row 2: Ch 1, turn; sc in each sc across to next ch-3 sp, 3 sc in ch-3 sp, sc in each sc across.

Row 3: Ch 1, turn; sc in each sc across; finish off.

Sew button to Left Front opposite button loop.

Openwork Jacket

◖■▢▢▷ EASY +

Size	Finished Chest Measurement
Extra Small	32$\frac{1}{2}$" (82.5 cm)
Small	37$\frac{1}{2}$" (95.5 cm)
Medium	40$\frac{1}{2}$" (103 cm)
Large	44$\frac{1}{4}$" (112.5 cm)
Extra Large	49$\frac{1}{4}$" (125 cm)
2X-Large	52$\frac{1}{4}$" (132.5 cm)
3X-Large	56" (142 cm)

Size Note: Instructions are written for size Extra Small with sizes Small, Medium, and Large in first set of braces { } and sizes Extra Large, 2X-Large, and 3X-Large in second set of braces. Instructions will be easier to read if you circle all the numbers pertaining to your size. If only one number is given, it applies to all sizes.

MATERIALS

Bulky Weight Yarn
[3.5 ounces, 155 yards
(100 grams, 142 meters) per skein]:
9{9-10-12}{13-14-16} skeins
Crochet hook, size N (9 mm) **or** size needed
for gauge
Split-ring markers - 4
Sewing needle and thread
1" (25 mm) Buttons - 3

GAUGE: In pattern, 20 dc = 6$\frac{3}{4}$" (17.25 cm);
4 rows = 4" (10 cm)

Gauge Swatch: 4" (10 cm) square
Ch 14.
Row 1: Dc in fourth ch from hook **(3 skipped chs count as first dc)** and in each ch across: 12 dc.
Rows 2-4: Ch 3 **(counts as first dc)**, turn; dc in next dc and in each dc across.
Finish off.

Instructions continued on page 68.

Jacket is crocheted in one piece from the neck down.

YOKE

Ch 46{50-50-54}{54-54-54}.

Row 1: Sc in second ch from hook and in each ch across: 45{49-49-53}{53-53-53} sc.

Row 2: Ch 1, turn; sc in each sc across increasing 0{0-4-4}{8-12-16} sc evenly spaced *(see Zeros, page 125)*: 45{49-53-57}{61-65-69} sc.

Row 3: Ch 3 **(counts as first dc, now and throughout)**, turn; 1{1-2-1}{1-2-1} dc in each of next 2 sc, skip next sc, 3 dc in next sc, ★ skip next sc, dc in next sc, skip next sc, 3 dc in next sc; repeat from ★ across to last 4 sc, skip next sc, 1{1-2-1}{1-2-1} dc in each of next 2 sc, dc in last sc: 45{49-57-57}{61-69-69} dc.

Row 4: Ch 3, turn; dc in next 2{2-4-2}{2-4-2} dc, skip next dc, 5 dc in next dc, ★ skip next dc, 2 dc in next dc, skip next dc, 5 dc in next dc; repeat from ★ across to last 4{4-6-4}{4-6-4} dc, skip next dc, dc in last 3{3-5-3}{3-5-3} dc: 74{81-92-95}{102-113-116} dc.

Row 5: Ch 3, turn; dc in next 2{2-4-2}{2-4-2} dc, skip next 2 dc, 5 dc in next dc, ★ skip next 2 dc, dc in next 2 dc, skip next 2 dc, 5 dc in next dc; repeat from ★ across to last 5{5-7-5}{5-7-5} dc, skip next 2 dc, dc in last 3{3-5-3}{3-5-3} dc.

Row 6: Ch 3, turn; dc in next 2{2-4-2}{2-4-2} dc, skip next 2 dc, 5 dc in next dc, ★ skip next 2 dc, 3 dc in each of next 2 dc, skip next 2 dc, 5 dc in next dc; repeat from ★ across to last 5{5-7-5}{5-7-5} dc, skip next 2 dc, dc in last 3{3-5-3}{3-5-3} dc: 110{121-136-143}{154-169-176} dc.

Row 7: Ch 3, turn; dc in next 2{2-4-2}{2-4-2} dc, skip next 2 dc, 5 dc in next dc, ★ skip next 3 dc, 3 dc in next dc, skip next 2 dc, 3 dc in next dc, skip next 3 dc, 5 dc in next dc; repeat from ★ across to last 5{5-7-5}{5-7-5} dc, skip next 2 dc, dc in last 3{3-5-3}{3-5-3} dc.

Row 8: Ch 3, turn; dc in next 2{2-4-2}{2-4-2} dc, skip next 2 dc, 5 dc in next dc, skip next 3 dc, 5 dc in next dc, skip next 2 dc, 3 dc in next dc, ★ (skip next 3 dc, 5 dc in next dc) twice, skip next 2 dc, 3 dc in next dc; repeat from ★ across to last 9{9-11-9}{9-11-9} dc, skip next 3 dc, 5 dc in next dc, skip next 2 dc, dc in last 3{3-5-3}{3-5-3} dc: 128{141-158-167}{180-197-206} dc.

Row 9: Ch 3, turn; dc in next 2{2-4-2}{2-4-2} dc, skip next 2 dc, 5 dc in next dc, ★ skip next 3 dc, 3 dc in next dc, skip next 3 dc, 5 dc in next dc, skip next 4 dc, 5 dc in next dc; repeat from ★ across to last 5{5-7-5}{5-7-5} dc, skip next 2 dc, dc in last 3{3-5-3}{3-5-3} dc.

Row 10: Ch 3, turn; dc in next 2{2-4-2}{2-4-2} dc, skip next 2 dc, 5 dc in next dc, ★ skip next 4 dc, 5 dc in next dc, (skip next 3 dc, 5 dc in next dc) twice; repeat from ★ across to last 5{5-7-5} {5-7-5} dc, skip next 2 dc, dc in last 3{3-5-3} {3-5-3} dc: 146{161-180-191}{206-225-236} dc.

Row 11: Ch 3, turn; dc in next 2{2-4-2}{2-4-2} dc, skip next 2 dc, 5 dc in next dc, (skip next 4 dc, 5 dc in next dc) across to last 5{5-7-5}{5-7-5} dc, skip next 2 dc, dc in last 3{3-5-3}{3-5-3} dc.

Sizes Extra Large, 2X-Large, & 3X-Large ONLY
Row 12: Repeat Row 11.

BODY
All Sizes
Row 1 (Right side)**:** Ch 3, turn; dc in next 2{2-4-2} {2-4-2} dc, skip next 2 dc, 5 dc in next dc, (skip next 4 dc, 5 dc in next dc) 3{4-4-5}{6-6-7} times, skip next dc, 3 dc in next dc (Left Front), skip next 30{30-35-35}{35-40-40} dc (armhole), 2 dc in next dc, place marker around first skipped dc and around last skipped dc, skip next dc, 5 dc in next dc, (skip next 4 dc, 5 dc in next dc) 7{8-9-10} {11-12-13} times, skip next dc, 2 dc in next dc (Back), skip next 30{30-35-35}{35-40-40} dc (armhole), 3 dc in next dc, place marker around first skipped dc and around last skipped dc, skip next dc, 5 dc in next dc, (skip next 4 dc, 5 dc in next dc) 3{4-4-5}{6-6-7} times, skip next 2 dc, dc in last 3{3-5-3}{3-5-3} sts (Right Front): 96{111-120-131}{146-155-166} dc.

Instructions continued on page 70.

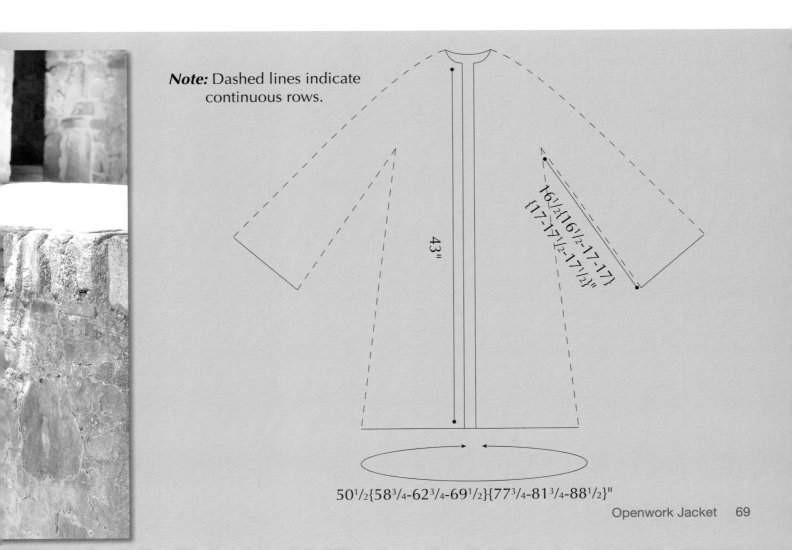

Note: Dashed lines indicate continuous rows.

43"

16½{16½-17-17} {17-17½-17½}"

50½{58¾-62¾-69½}{77¾-81¾-88½}"

Note: Loop a short piece of yarn around any stitch to mark Row 1 as **right** side.

Row 2: Ch 3, turn; dc in next 2{2-4-2}{2-4-2} dc, skip next 2 dc, (3 dc, ch 1, 3 dc) in next dc, ★ skip next 4 dc, (3 dc, ch 1, 3 dc) in next dc; repeat from ★ across to last 5{5-7-5}{5-7-5} dc, dc in last 3{3-5-3}{3-5-3} dc: 114{132-142-156}{174-184-198} dc and 18{21-22-25}{28-29-32} ch-1 sps.

Rows 3-9: Ch 3, turn; dc in next 2{2-4-2}{2-4-2} dc, (3 dc, ch 1, 3 dc) in each ch-1 sp across to last 6{6-8-6}{6-8-6} dc, skip next 3 dc, dc in last 3{3-5-3}{3-5-3} dc.

Row 10: Ch 3, turn; dc in next 2{2-4-2}{2-4-2} dc, (4 dc, ch 1, 4 dc) in each ch-1 sp across to last 6{6-8-6}{6-8-6} dc, skip next 3 dc, dc in last 3{3-5-3}{3-5-3} dc: 150{174-186-206}{230-242-262} dc and 18{21-22-25}{28-29-32} ch-1 sps.

Row 11: Ch 3, turn; dc in next 2{2-4-2}{2-4-2} dc, (4 dc, ch 1, 4 dc) in each ch-1 sp across to last 7{7-9-7}{7-9-7} dc, skip next 4 dc, dc in last 3{3-5-3}{3-5-3} dc.

Repeat Row 11 for pattern until piece measures approximately 43" (109 cm) from beginning ch, ending by working a **right** side row.

Finish off.

SLEEVE

Rnd 1: With **right** side facing, join yarn with dc in first marked dc of either armhole **(see Joining With Dc, page 125)**; 5 dc in same st, skip next dc, 5 dc in next dc, (skip next 4 dc, 5 dc in next dc) 5{5-6-6}{6-7-7} times, skip next dc, 6 dc in next marked dc; join with slip st to first dc: 42{42-47-47}{47-52-52} dc.

Rnd 2: Ch 3, turn; dc in next dc, skip next 2 dc, 5 dc in next dc, (skip next 4 dc, 5 dc in next dc) around to last 2 dc, skip last 2 dc; join with slip st to first dc.

Rnd 3: Ch 3, turn; skip next 2 dc, 5 dc in next dc, (skip next 4 dc, 5 dc in next dc) around to last 3 dc, skip next 2 dc, dc in last dc; join with slip st to first dc.

Repeat Rnds 2 and 3 for pattern until Sleeve measures approximately 16½{16½-17-17}{17-17½-17½}"/42{42-43-43}{43-44.5-44.5} cm from beginning of Rnd 1, ending by working a **right** side row.

Finish off.

Repeat for second Sleeve.

FINISHING
LEFT FRONT EDGING
With **right** side facing and working in end of rows across Left Front, join yarn with dc in first ch at base of first sc on Row 1 of Yoke; dc in first sc row, ★ skip next 2 rows, 4 dc in next row; repeat from ★ across, skip first dc on last row, 4 dc in next dc, slip st in next dc; finish off.

RIGHT FRONT EDGING
With **right** side facing and beginning on bottom edge, join yarn with slip st in fourth dc from Right Front edge; skip next dc, 4 dc in next dc; working in end of rows across Right Front, 4 dc in first row, ★ skip next 2 rows, 4 dc in next row; repeat from ★ across to last 3 rows, skip next 2 rows, dc in last sc row and in next ch; finish off.

Using photo as a guide, sew buttons to Left Front. Use spaces between 4-dc groups as buttonholes.

Best Bouclé Cardigan

■■□□ **EASY +**

Shown on page 73.

Size	Finished Chest Measurement
Extra Small/Small	33½" (85 cm)
Medium/Large	41" (104 cm)
Extra Large/2X-Large	51" (129.5 cm)

Size Note: Instructions are written for size Extra Small/Small with sizes Medium/Large and Extra Large/2X-Large in braces { }. Instructions will be easier to read if you circle all the numbers pertaining to your size. If only one number is given, it applies to all sizes.

MATERIALS

Medium Weight Yarn
[1¾ ounces, 90 yards
(50 grams, 83 meters) per ball]:
    Variegated - 11{13-15} balls
    Red - 8{9-11} skeins
Crochet hook, size J (6 mm) **or** size needed
  for gauge
Yarn needle
Sewing needle and thread
⅞" (22 mm) Button

GAUGE: In pattern,
    16 sts and 20 rows = 4" (10 cm)

Gauge Swatch: 4¼" (10.75 cm) square
With Variegated, ch 18.
Rows 1-21: Work same as Back, page 72: 17 sts.
Finish off.

STITCH GUIDE

FRONT POST TREBLE CROCHET
  (abbreviated FPtr)
YO twice, insert hook from **front** to **back** around post of st indicated *(Fig. 4, page 126)*, YO and pull up a loop (4 loops on hook), (YO and draw through 2 loops on hook) 3 times. Skip sc behind FPtr.
DECREASE
Pull up a loop in each of next 2 sc, YO and draw through all 3 loops on hook **(counts as one sc)**.

Instructions continued on page 72.

BACK

With Variegated, ch 68{83-103}.

Row 1 (Right side): Sc in second ch from hook and in each ch across: 67{82-102} sc.

Note: Loop a short piece of yarn around any stitch to mark Row 1 as **right** side.

Row 2: Ch 1, turn; sc in each sc across changing to Red in last sc **(Fig. 3, page 126)**.

Carry unused color along side of piece.

Row 3: Ch 1, turn; sc in each sc across.

Row 4: Ch 1, turn; sc in each sc across changing to Variegated in last sc.

Row 5: Ch 1, turn; sc in first 3 sc, work FPtr around sc two rows **below** next sc, ★ sc in next 4 sc on previous row, work FPtr around sc two rows **below** next sc; repeat from ★ across to last 3 sc on previous row, sc in last 3 sc.

Row 6: Ch 1, turn; sc in each st across changing to Red in last sc.

Row 7: Ch 1, turn; sc in each sc across.

Row 8: Ch 1, turn; sc in each sc across changing to Variegated in last sc.

Row 9: Ch 1, turn; sc in first 3 sc, work FPtr around next FPtr, ★ sc in next 4 sc, work FPtr around next FPtr; repeat from ★ across to last 3 sc, sc in last 3 sc.

Repeat Rows 6-9 for pattern until piece measures approximately 14½" (37 cm) from beginning ch, ending by working Row 9; cut Red.

Last Row: Ch 1, turn; sc in each st across; finish off leaving a long length for sewing underarm.

SLEEVE (Make 2)

With Variegated and leaving a long end for sewing, ch 58{63-68}.

Work same as for Back until Sleeve measures approximately 10" (25.5 cm) from beginning ch, ending by working Row 9; cut Red: 57{62-67} sts.

Last Row: Ch 1, turn; sc in each st across; finish off leaving a long length for sewing underarm.

LEFT FRONT

With Variegated, ch 38{48-58}.

Work same as for Back: 37{47-57} sts.

RIGHT FRONT

With Variegated, ch 38{48-58}.

Work same as for Back, ending by working Row 6; do **not** cut either yarn: 37{47-57} sts.

YOKE

Row 1 (Joining row): With **right** side of Right Front facing, sc in each sc across to last 6{11-11} sc, leave remaining sc unworked on Right Front for armhole; with **right** side of one Sleeve facing, skip first 6{11-11} sc, sc in next sc and in each sc across to last 6{11-11} sc, leave remaining sc unworked on Sleeve; with **right** side of Back facing, skip first 6{11-11} sc, sc in next sc and in each sc across to last 6{11-11} sc, leave remaining sc unworked on Back; with **right** side of remaining Sleeve facing, skip first 6{11-11} sc, sc in next sc and in each sc across to last 6{11-11} sc, leave remaining sc unworked on Sleeve; with **right** side of Left Front facing, skip first 6{11-11} sc, sc in next sc and in each sc across: 207{212-262} sc.

Row 2: Ch 1, turn; sc in each sc across changing to Variegated in last sc.

Instructions continued on page 74.

Row 3: Ch 1, turn; sc in first 3 sc, work FPtr around next FPtr, ★ sc in next 4 sc, work FPtr around next FPtr; repeat from ★ across to last 3 sc, sc in last 3 sc.

Row 4: Ch 1, turn; sc in each st across changing to Red in last sc.

Row 5: Ch 1, turn; sc in each sc across.

Row 6: Ch 1, turn; sc in each sc across changing to Variegated in last sc.

Rows 7-18: Repeat Rows 3-6, 3 times.

Row 19: Ch 1, turn; sc in first 3 sc, work FPtr around next FPtr, ★ sc in next sc, decrease, sc in next sc, work FPtr around next FPtr; repeat from ★ across to last 3 sc, sc in last 3 sc: 167{171-211} sc.

Rows 20-22: Repeat Rows 4-6.

Row 23: Ch 1, turn; sc in first 3 sc, work FPtr around next FPtr, ★ sc in next sc, decrease, work FPtr around next FPtr; repeat from ★ across to last 3 sc, sc in last 3 sc: 127{130-160} sc.

Rows 24-26: Repeat Rows 4-6.

Row 27: Ch 1, turn; sc in first 3 sc, work FPtr around next FPtr, ★ decrease, work FPtr around next FPtr; repeat from ★ across to last 3 sc, sc in last 3 sc: 87{89-109} sc.

Rows 28-30: Repeat Rows 4-6.

Row 31: Ch 1, turn; sc in first 3 sc, work FPtr around next FPtr, ★ sc in next sc, work FPtr around next FPtr; repeat from ★ across to last 3 sc, sc in last 3 sc.

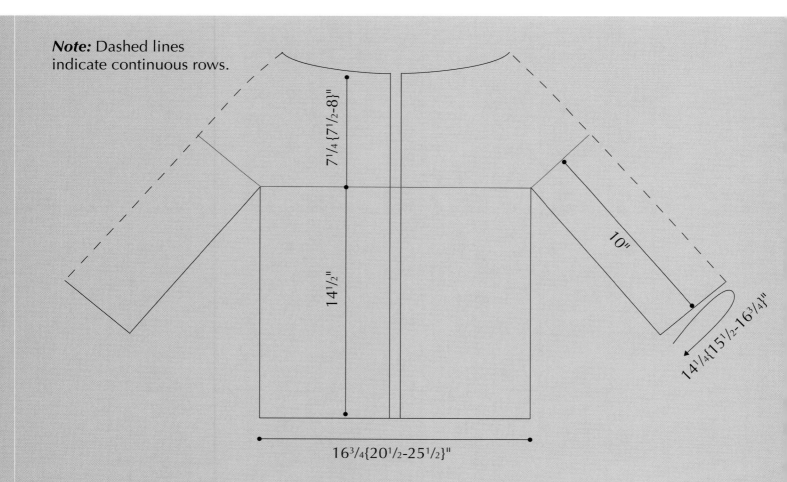

Note: Dashed lines indicate continuous rows.

7¹⁄₄{7¹⁄₂-8}"

14¹⁄₂"

10"

14¹⁄₄{15¹⁄₂-16³⁄₄}"

16³⁄₄{20¹⁄₂-25¹⁄₂}"

Rows 32 thru 36{36-40}: Repeat Rows 28-31, 1{1-2} time(s); then repeat Row 4.

Extra Small/Small & Extra Large/2X-Large ONLY
Finish off both yarns.

Medium/Large ONLY
Rows 37 and 38: Repeat Rows 5 and 6.

Finish off both yarns.

FINISHING
BAND
With **right** side facing and working in end of rows, join Red with sc at Right Front bottom corner; sc evenly across Right Front edge; working across neck edge, 2 sc in first sc; sc tightly in each sc across to last sc, 2 sc in last sc; working in end of rows, sc evenly across Left Front edge; finish off.

BUTTON LOOP
With **wrong** side of Right Front facing and working behind Band, join Red with slip st in top corner, ch 6, skip next 6 rows, slip st in next row; finish off.

Using long end at underarm, whipstitch unworked stitches on Sleeves to Back and Fronts *(Fig. 7, page 127)*.

Weave Sleeve and side in one continuous seam *(Fig. 6, page 127)*.

Sew button to Left Front opposite Button Loop.

Belted Pant Coat

■■□□ EASY

Size	Finished Chest Measurement	
Extra Small	33"	(84 cm)
Small	38"	(96.5 cm)
Medium	42"	(106.5 cm)
Large	46"	(117 cm)
Extra Large	49"	(124.5 cm)
2X-Large	54"	(137 cm)
3X-Large	57"	(145 cm)

Size Note: Instructions are written for size Extra Small with sizes Small, Medium, and Large in first set of braces { } and sizes Extra Large, 2X-Large, and 3X-Large in second set of braces. Instructions will be easier to read if you circle all the numbers pertaining to your size. If only one number is given, it applies to all sizes.

MATERIALS

Medium Weight Yarn
[3.5 ounces, 196 yards
(100 grams, 179 meters) per skein]:
8{8-9-9}{10-10-11} skeins
Crochet hook, size J (6 mm) **or** size needed
for gauge
Yarn needle
Sewing needle and thread
1¼" (32 mm) Buttons - 2

GAUGE: 12 dc and 7 rows = 4" (10 cm)

Gauge Swatch: 4" (10 cm) square
Ch 13.
Row 1: Dc in third ch from hook **(2 skipped chs count as first dc)** and in each ch across: 12 dc.
Rows 2-7: Ch 3 **(counts as first dc)**, turn; dc in next dc and in each dc across.
Finish off.

Instructions continued on page 78.

STITCH GUIDE

DECREASE (uses next 2 sts)
★ YO, insert hook in **next** st, YO and pull up a loop, YO and draw through 2 loops on hook; repeat from ★ once **more**, YO and draw through all 3 loops on hook **(counts as one dc)**.

BACK

Ch 51{58-64-70}{75-82-87}.

Row 1 (Right side): Dc in third ch from hook **(2 skipped chs count as first dc)** and in each ch across: 50{57-63-69}{74-81-86} dc.

Note: Loop a short piece of yarn around any stitch to mark Row 1 as **right** side.

Rows 2-32: Ch 2 **(counts as first dc, now and throughout)**, turn; dc in next dc and in each dc across.

ARMHOLE SHAPING

Row 1: Turn; slip st in first 3{4-5-6}{7-8-9} dc, ch 2, dc in next dc and in each dc to last 2{3-4-5}{6-7-8} dc, leave remaining dc unworked: 46{51-55-59}{62-67-70} dc.

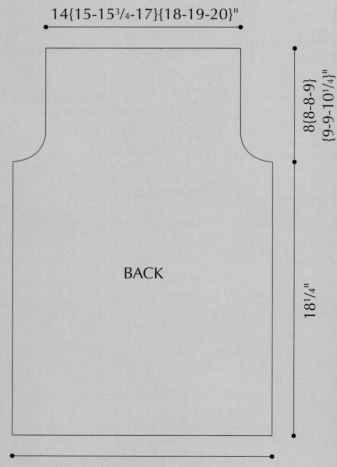

14{15-15³⁄₄-17}{18-19-20}"

8{8-8-9}
{9-9-10¹⁄₄}"

BACK

18¹⁄₄"

16¹⁄₂{19-21-23}{24¹⁄₂-27-28¹⁄₂}"

Row 2: Turn; slip st in first 3{4-5-5}{5-6-6} dc, ch 2, dc in next dc and in each dc across to last 2{3-4-4}{4-5-5} dc, leave remaining dc unworked: 42{45-47-51}{54-57-60} dc.

Rows 3 thru 14{14-14-16}{16-16-18}: Ch 2, turn; dc in next dc and in each dc across.

Finish off.

LEFT FRONT
Ch 40{43-46-49}{52-55-58}.

Row 1 (Right side): Dc in third ch from hook **(2 skipped chs count as first dc)** and in each ch across: 39{42-45-48}{51-54-57} dc.

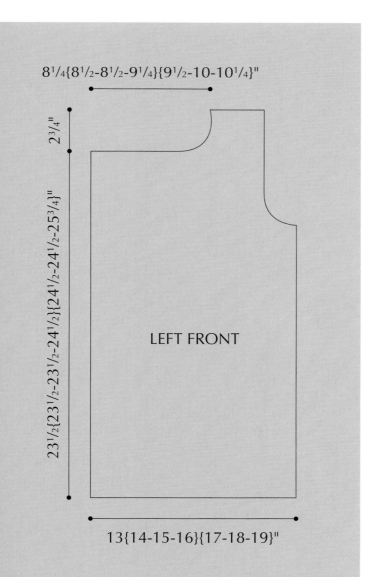

8¹/₄{8¹/₂-8¹/₂-9¹/₄}{9¹/₂-10-10¹/₄}"

2³/₄"

23¹/₂{23¹/₂-23¹/₂-24¹/₂}{24¹/₂-24¹/₂-25³/₄}"

LEFT FRONT

13{14-15-16}{17-18-19}"

Note: Mark Row 1 as **right** side.

Rows 2-32: Ch 2, turn; dc in next dc and in each dc across.

ARMHOLE SHAPING
Row 1: Turn; slip st in first 3{4-5-6}{7-8-9} dc, ch 2, dc in next dc and in each dc across: 37{39-41-43}{45-47-49} dc.

Row 2: Ch 2, turn; dc in next dc and in each dc across to last 2{3-4-4}{4-5-5} dc, leave remaining sts unworked: 35{36-37-39}{41-42-44} dc.

Rows 3 thru 9{9-9-11}{11-11-13}: Ch 2, turn; dc next dc and in each dc across.

Finish off.

NECK SHAPING
Row 1: With **wrong** side facing, skip first 20{21-21-23}{24-25-26} dc and join yarn with dc in next dc **(see *Joining With Dc, page 125)***, dc in next dc and in each dc across: 15{15-16-16}{17-17-18} dc.

Row 2: Ch 2, turn; dc in next 13{13-14-14}{15-15-16} dc, leave remaining dc unworked: 14{14-15-15}{16-16-17} dc.

Row 3: Turn; slip st in first 3 dc, ch 2, dc in next dc and in each dc across: 12{12-13-13}{14-14-15} dc.

Row 4: Ch 2, turn; dc in next 9{9-10-10}{11-11-12} dc, leave remaining dc unworked: 10{10-11-11}{12-12-13} dc.

Row 5: Ch 2, turn; dc in next dc and in each dc across; finish off leaving a long for sewing.

Instructions continued on page 80.

RIGHT FRONT

Work same as Left Front to Armhole Shaping:
39{42-45-48}{51-54-57} dc.

ARMHOLE SHAPING

Row 1: Ch 2, turn; dc in next dc and in each dc
across to last 2{3-4-5}{6-7-8} dc, leave remaining
dc unworked: 37{39-41-43}{45-47-49} dc.

Row 2: Turn; slip st in first 3{4-5-5}{5-6-6} dc,
ch 2, dc in next dc and in each dc across:
35{36-37-39}{41-42-44} dc.

Rows 3 thru 9{9-9-11}{11-11-13}: Ch 2, turn; dc
in next dc and in each dc across.

NECK SHAPING

Row 1: Ch 2, turn; dc in next 14{14-15-15}
{16-16-17} dc, leaving remaining dc unworked:
15{15-16-16}{17-17-18} dc.

Row 2: Turn; slip st in first 2 dc, ch 2, dc in next
dc and in each dc across:
14{14-15-15}{16-16-17} dc.

Row 3: Ch 2, turn; dc in next 11{11-12-12}
{13-13-14} dc, leaving remaining dc unworked:
12{12-13-13}{14-14-15} dc.

Row 4: Turn; slip st in first 3 dc, ch 2, dc in next
dc and in each dc across: 10{10-11-11}
{12-12-13} dc.

Row 5: Ch 2, turn; dc in next dc and in each dc
across; finish off leaving a long for sewing.

SLEEVE (Make 2)

Ch 48{49-50-51}{52-53-54}.

Row 1 (Right side): Dc in third ch from hook **(2 skipped chs count as first dc)** and in each ch across: 47{48-49-50}{51-52-53} dc.

Note: Mark Row 1 as **right** side.

Row 2: Ch 2, turn; dc in next dc and in each dc across.

Row 3 (Decrease row): Ch 2, turn; decrease, dc in next dc and in each dc across to last 3 dc, decrease, dc in last dc: 45{46-47-48} {49-50-51} dc.

Rows 4 and 5: Ch 2, turn; dc in next dc and in each dc across.

Rows 6-18: Repeat Rows 3-5, 4 times; then repeat Row 3 once **more**: 35{36-37-38}{39-40-41} dc.

Rows 19-29: Ch 2, turn; dc in next dc and in each dc across.

CAP SHAPING

Row 1: Turn; slip st in first 4 dc, ch 2, dc in next dc and in each dc across to last 3 dc, leave remaining dc unworked: 29{30-31-32}{33-34-35} dc.

Row 2: Turn; slip st in first 3 dc, ch 2, dc in next dc and in each dc across to last 2 dc, leave remaining dc unworked: 25{26-27-28}{29-30-31} dc.

Instructions continued on page 82.

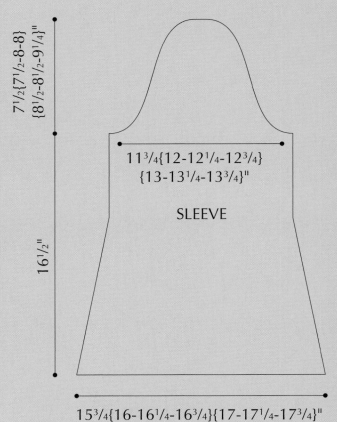

7¹/₂{7¹/₂-8-8}{8¹/₂-8¹/₂-9¹/₄}"

11³/₄{12-12¹/₄-12³/₄} {13-13¹/₄-13³/₄}"

SLEEVE

16¹/₂"

15³/₄{16-16¹/₄-16³/₄}{17-17¹/₄-17³/₄}"

Rows 3 and 4: Ch 2, turn; dc in next dc and in each dc across.

Row 5 (Decrease row)**:** Ch 2, turn; decrease, dc in next dc and in each dc across to last 3 dc, decrease, dc in last dc: 23{24-25-26}{27-28-29} dc.

Rows 6-8: Repeat Rows 3-5: 21{22-23-24}{25-26-27} dc.

Rows 9 thru 10{10-11-11}{12-12-13}: Ch 2, turn; dc in next dc and in each dc across.

Next 2 Rows: Turn; slip st in first 4 dc, ch 2, dc in next dc and in each dc across to last 3 dc, leave remaining sts unworked: 9{10-11-12}{13-14-15} dc.

Last Row: Turn; slip st in first 3 dc, ch 2, dc in next dc and in each dc across to last 2 dc, leave remaining dc unworked; finish off: 5{6-7-8}{9-10-11} dc.

BELT LOOPS (Make 4)
Ch 5.

Row 1: Sc in second ch from hook and in each ch across: 4 sc.

Rows 2-9: Ch 1, turn; sc in each sc across.

Finish off leaving a long end for sewing.

FINISHING
Whipstitch shoulder seams *(Fig. 7, page 127)*.

Weave Sleeves to Coat *(Fig. 6, page 127)*.

Weave underarm and side in one continuous seam.

Sew Belt Loops to Coat each 4" (10 cm) from side seams and beginning 9½" (24 cm) from bottom edge.

COLLAR
With **right** side facing, skip first 12 dc from Right Front edge and join yarn with sc in next dc *(see Joining With Sc, page 125)*; work 12{13-13-15}{16-17-18} sc evenly spaced across, work 22{25-25-29}{30-33-34} sc evenly spaced across Back neck edge, work 13{14-14-16}{17-18-19} sc evenly spaced across Left Front neck edge to last 12 dc, leave remaining dc unworked: 48{53-53-61}{64-69-72} sc.

Row 1: Ch 2, turn; dc across increasing 12 dc evenly spaced *(see Increasing Evenly Across A Row, page 126)*: 60{65-65-73}{76-81-84} dc.

Row 2: Ch 2, turn; dc in next dc and in each dc across.

Row 3: Ch 2, turn; dc across increasing 6 dc evenly spaced: 66{71-71-79}{82-87-90} dc.

Row 4: Ch 2, turn; dc in next dc and in each dc across.

Row 5: Ch 2, turn; dc across increasing 6 dc evenly spaced: 72{77-77-85} {88-93-96} dc.

Rows 6-9: Ch 2, turn; dc in next dc and in each dc across.

Finish off.

FRONT & COLLAR EDGING

Row 1: With **right** side facing, join yarn with sc in Right Front bottom corner; sc evenly across to Left Front bottom corner, increasing and decreasing to keep edges from ruffling.

Row 2: Ch 1, do **not** turn; working from **left** to **right**, work reverse sc in each sc across *(Figs. 8a-d, page 127)*; finish off.

Sew buttons to Left Front using spaces between sts as buttonholes.

Weekend Warmer Sweater

◼◼◼◻ **INTERMEDIATE**

Size	Finished Chest Measurement
Extra Small	31" (78.5 cm)
Small	36" (91.5 cm)
Medium	41" (104 cm)
Large	46" (117 cm)
Extra Large	51" (129.5 cm)
2X-Large	56" (142 cm)
3X-Large	61" (155 cm)

Size Note: Instructions are written for size Extra Small with sizes Small, Medium, and Large in first set of braces { } and sizes Extra Large, 2X-Large, and 3X-Large in second set of braces. Instructions will be easier to read if you circle all the numbers pertaining to your size. If only one number is given, it applies to all sizes.

MATERIALS

Medium Weight Yarn
[1.5 ounces, 84 yards
(40 grams, 71 meters) per ball]:
15{16-17-18}{19-20-21} balls
Crochet hooks, sizes G (4 mm) **and** I (5.5 mm)
or sizes needed for gauge
Yarn needle
Sewing needle and thread
³/₄" (19 mm) Buttons - 10
T-pins

GAUGE: With larger size hook, in pattern,
(Shell, FPdc) 4 times (24 sts) =
5" (12.75 cm); 7 rows = 4" (10 cm)

Gauge Swatch: 5¹/₂"w x 4¹/₂"h (14 cm x 11.5 cm)
With larger size hook, ch 28.
Work Rows 1-8 of Back, page 86.
Finish off.

Instructions continued on page 86.

STITCH GUIDE

SHELL
(2 Dc, ch 1, 2 dc) in st or sp indicated.

FRONT POST DOUBLE CROCHET
(abbreviated FPdc)
YO, insert hook from **front** to **back** around post of st indicated *(Fig. 4, page 126)*, YO and pull up a loop (3 loops on hook), (YO and draw through 2 loops on hook) twice.

BACK POST DOUBLE CROCHET
(abbreviated BPdc)
YO, insert hook from **back** to **front** around post of st indicated *(Fig. 4, page 126)*, YO and pull up a loop (3 loops on hook), (YO and draw through 2 loops on hook) twice.

BACK

With larger size hook,
ch 76{88-100-112}{124-136-148}.

Row 1 (Right side): Sc in second ch from hook and in each ch across: 75{87-99-111}{123-135-147} sc.

Note: Loop a short piece of yarn around any stitch to mark Row 1 as **right** side.

Row 2: Ch 3 **(counts as first dc, now and throughout)**, turn; dc in next sc, skip next 2 sc, work Shell in next sc, ★ skip next 2 sc, dc in next sc, skip next 2 sc, work Shell in next sc; repeat from ★ across to last 4 sc, skip next 2 sc, dc in last 2 sc: 12{14-16-18}{20-22-24} Shells.

Row 3: Ch 3, turn; work FPdc around next dc, ★ work Shell in next ch-1 sp, skip next 2 dc, work FPdc around next dc; repeat from ★ across to last dc, dc in last dc.

Row 4: Ch 3, turn; work BPdc around next FPdc, ★ work Shell in next ch-1 sp, work BPdc around next FPdc; repeat from ★ across to last dc, dc in last dc.

Row 5: Ch 3, turn; work FPdc around next BPdc, ★ work Shell in next ch-1 sp, work FPdc around next BPdc; repeat from ★ across to last dc, dc in last dc.

Rows 6-26: Repeat Rows 4 and 5, 10 times; then repeat Row 4 once **more**.

ARMHOLE SHAPING

Row 1: Turn; working in sts and in chs, slip st in first 5{5-5-5}{11-11-11} sts, ch 3, dc in next 2 dc, work FPdc around next BPdc, ★ work Shell in next ch-1 sp, work FPdc around next BPdc; repeat from ★ 9{11-13-15}{15-17-19} times **more**, dc in next 2 dc and in next ch-1 sp, leave remaining sts unworked: 10{12-14-16}{16-18-20} Shells and 6 dc.

Row 2: Turn; slip st in first 3 dc, ch 3, work BPdc around next FPdc, ★ work Shell in next ch-1 sp, work BPdc around next FPdc; repeat from ★ across to last 3 dc, dc in next dc, leave remaining dc unworked: 10{12-14-16}{16-18-20} Shells and 2 dc.

Sizes Extra Small & Small ONLY

Row 3: Ch 3, turn; work FPdc around next BPdc, ★ work Shell in next ch-1 sp, work FPdc around next BPdc; repeat from ★ across to last dc, dc in last dc.

Row 4: Ch 3, turn; work BPdc around next FPdc, ★ work Shell in next ch-1 sp, work BPdc around next FPdc; repeat from ★ across to last dc, dc in last dc.

Rows 5-16: Repeat Rows 3 and 4, 6 times.

Finish off.

Sizes Medium, Large, Extra Large, 2X-Large, & 3X-Large ONLY

Row 3: Turn; working in sts and in chs, slip st in first {5-5}{5-5-11} sts, ch 3, dc in next 2 dc, work FPdc around next BPdc, ★ work Shell in next ch-1 sp, work FPdc around next BPdc; repeat from ★ {11-13}{13-15-15} times **more**, dc in next 2 dc and in next ch-1 sp, leave remaining sts unworked: {12-14}{14-16-16} Shells and 6 dc.

Row 4: Turn; slip st in first 3 dc, ch 3, work BPdc around next FPdc, ★ work Shell in next ch-1 sp, work BPdc around next FPdc; repeat from ★ across to last 3 dc, dc in next dc, leave remaining dc unworked: {12-14}{14-16-16} Shells and 2 dc.

Row 5: Ch 3, turn; work FPdc around next BPdc, ★ work Shell in next ch-1 sp, work FPdc around next BPdc; repeat from ★ across to last dc, dc in last dc.

Instructions continued on page 88.

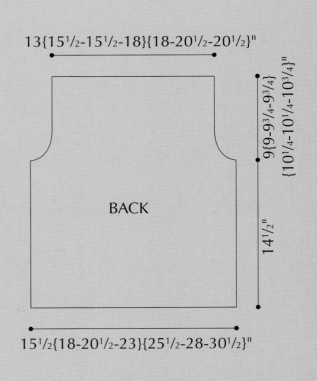

13{15½-15½-18}{18-20½-20½}"

9{9-9¾-9¾}{10¼-10¼-10¾}"

14½"

BACK

15½{18-20½-23}{25½-28-30½}"

Row 6: Ch 3, turn; work BPdc around next FPdc, ★ work Shell in next ch-1 sp, work BPdc around next FPdc; repeat from ★ across to last dc, dc in last dc.

Rows 7 thru {17-17}{18-18-19}: Repeat Rows 5 and 6, {5-5}{6-6-6} times; then repeat Row 5, {1-1}{0-0-1} time(s) **more** *(see Zeros, page 125)*.

Finish off.

LEFT FRONT
With larger size hook,
ch 34{40-46-52}{58-64-70}.

Work same as Back, page 86, to Armhole Shaping: 5{6-7-8}{9-10-11} Shells.

ARMHOLE SHAPING
Row 1: Turn; working in sts and in chs, slip st in first 5{5-5-5}{11-11-11} sts, ch 3, dc in next 2 dc, work FPdc around next BPdc, ★ work Shell in next ch-1 sp, work FPdc around next BPdc; repeat from ★ across to last dc, dc in last dc: 4{5-6-7}{7-8-9} Shells and 4 dc.

Row 2: Ch 3, turn; work BPdc around next FPdc, ★ work Shell in next ch-1 sp, work BPdc around next FPdc; repeat from ★ across to last 3 dc, dc in next dc, leave remaining dc unworked: 4{5-6-7}{7-8-9} Shells and 2 dc.

Sizes Extra Small & Small ONLY
Row 3: Ch 3, turn; work FPdc around next BPdc, ★ work Shell in next ch-1 sp, work FPdc around next BPdc; repeat from ★ across to last dc, dc in last dc.

Row 4: Ch 3, turn; work BPdc around next FPdc, ★ work Shell in next ch-1 sp, work BPdc around next FPdc; repeat from ★ across to last dc, dc in last dc.

Rows 5-8: Repeat Rows 3 and 4 twice.

Sizes Medium, Large, Extra Large, 2X-Large, & 3X-Large ONLY
Row 3: Turn; working in sts and in chs, slip st in first {5-5}{5-5-11} sts, ch 3, dc in next 2 dc, work FPdc around next BPdc, ★ work Shell in next ch-1 sp, work FPdc around next BPdc; repeat from ★ across to last dc, dc in last dc: {5-6}{6-7-7} Shells and 4 dc.

Row 4: Ch 3, turn; work BPdc around next FPdc, ★ work Shell in next ch-1 sp, work BPdc around next FPdc; repeat from ★ across to last 3 dc, dc in next dc, leave remaining dc unworked: {5-6}{6-7-7} Shells and 2 dc.

Row 5: Ch 3, turn; work FPdc around next BPdc, ★ work Shell in next ch-1 sp, work FPdc around next BPdc; repeat from ★ across to last dc, dc in last dc.

Row 6: Ch 3, turn; work BPdc around next FPdc, ★ work Shell in next ch-1 sp, work BPdc around next FPdc; repeat from ★ across to last dc, dc in last dc.

Rows 7-10: Repeat Rows 5 and 6 twice.

NECK SHAPING
All Sizes
Row 1: Ch 3, turn; work FPdc around next BPdc, ★ work Shell in next ch-1 sp, work FPdc around next BPdc; repeat from ★ 2{3-3-4}{4-5-5} times **more**, dc in next 2 dc, hdc in next ch-1 sp, leave remaining sts unworked: 3{4-4-5}{5-6-6} Shells.

Row 2: Turn; slip st in first 3 sts, ch 3, work BPdc around next FPdc, ★ work Shell in next ch-1 sp, work BPdc around next FPdc; repeat from ★ across to last dc, dc in last dc.

Row 3: Ch 3, turn; work FPdc around next BPdc, ★ work Shell in next ch-1 sp, work FPdc around next BPdc; repeat from ★ 1{2-2-3}{3-4-4} time(s) **more**, dc in next 2 dc, hdc in next ch-1 sp, leave remaining sts unworked: 2{3-3-4}{4-5-5} Shells.

Row 4: Turn; slip st in first 3 sts, ch 3, work BPdc around next FPdc, ★ work Shell in next ch-1 sp, work BPdc around next FPdc; repeat from ★ across to last dc, dc in last dc.

Size Extra Small ONLY
Row 5: Ch 3, turn; work FPdc around next BPdc, work Shell in next ch-1 sp, work FPdc around next BPdc, dc in next 2 dc, hdc in next ch-1 sp, leave remaining sts unworked: one Shell.

Row 6: Ch 3, turn; dc in next 2 dc, work BPdc around next FPdc, work Shell in next ch-1 sp, work BPdc around next FPdc, dc in last dc.

Row 7: Ch 3, turn; work FPdc around next BPdc, work Shell in next ch-1 sp, work FPdc around next BPdc, dc in last 3 dc.

Row 8: Repeat Row 6; finish off.

Sizes Small, Medium, Large, Extra Large, 2X-Large & 3X-Large ONLY
Row 5: Ch 3, turn; work FPdc around next BPdc, ★ work Shell in next ch-1 sp, work FPdc around next BPdc; repeat from ★ {1-1-2}{2-3-3} time(s) **more**, dc in next 2 dc, hdc in next ch-1 sp, leave remaining sts unworked: {2-2-3}{3-4-4} Shells.

Row 6: Turn; slip st in first 3 sts, ch 3, work BPdc around next FPdc, ★ work Shell in next ch-1 sp, work BPdc around next FPdc; repeat from ★ across to last dc, dc in last dc.

Sizes Small, Medium, Large, & Extra Large ONLY
Row 7: Ch 3, turn; work FPdc around next BPdc, ★ work Shell in next ch-1 sp, work FPdc around next BPdc; repeat from ★ across to last dc, dc in last dc.

Sizes Medium & Large ONLY
Finish off.

Instructions continued on page 90.

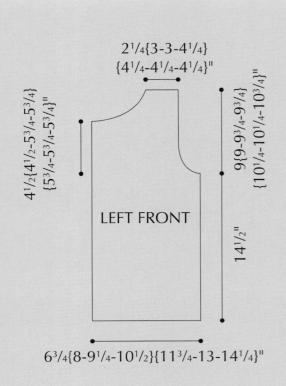

$2^{1}/_{4}\{3\text{-}3\text{-}4^{1}/_{4}\}$
$\{4^{1}/_{4}\text{-}4^{1}/_{4}\text{-}4^{1}/_{4}\}$"

$4^{1}/_{2}\{4^{1}/_{2}\text{-}5^{3}/_{4}\text{-}5^{3}/_{4}\}$
$\{5^{3}/_{4}\text{-}5^{3}/_{4}\text{-}5^{3}/_{4}\}$"

$9\{9\text{-}9^{3}/_{4}\text{-}9^{3}/_{4}\}$
$\{10^{1}/_{4}\text{-}10^{1}/_{4}\text{-}10^{3}/_{4}\}$"

$14^{1}/_{2}$"

LEFT FRONT

$6^{3}/_{4}\{8\text{-}9^{1}/_{4}\text{-}10^{1}/_{2}\}\{11^{3}/_{4}\text{-}13\text{-}14^{1}/_{4}\}$"

Sizes Small & Extra Large ONLY

Row 8: Ch 3, turn; work BPdc around next FPdc, ★ work Shell in next ch-1 sp, work BPdc around next FPdc; repeat from ★ across to last dc, dc in last dc; finish off.

Sizes 2X-Large & 3X-Large ONLY

Row 7: Ch 3, turn; work FPdc around next BPdc, ★ work Shell in next ch-1 sp, work FPdc around next BPdc; repeat from ★ 2 times **more**, dc in next 2 dc, hdc in next ch-1 sp, leave remaining sts unworked: 3 Shells.

Row 8: Turn; slip st in first 3 sts, ch 3, work BPdc around next FPdc, ★ work Shell in next ch-1 sp, work BPdc around next FPdc; repeat from ★ across to last dc, dc in last dc.

Size 2X-Large ONLY
Finish off.

Size 3X ONLY

Row 9: Ch 3, turn; work FPdc around next BPdc, ★ work Shell in next ch-1 sp, work FPdc around next BPdc; repeat from ★ across to last dc, dc in last dc; finish off.

RIGHT FRONT
With larger size hook,
ch 34{40-46-52}{58-64-70}.

Work same as Back, page 86, to Armhole Shaping: 5{6-7-8}{9-10-11} Shells.

ARMHOLE SHAPING

Row 1: Ch 3, turn; work FPdc around next BPdc, ★ work Shell in next ch-1 sp, work FPdc around next BPdc; repeat from ★ 3{4-5-6}{6-7-8} times **more**, dc in next 2 dc and in next ch-1 sp, leave remaining sts unworked: 4{5-6-7}{7-8-9} Shells and 4 dc.

Row 2: Turn; slip st in first 3 sts, ch 3, work BPdc around next FPdc, ★ work Shell in next ch-1 sp, work BPdc around next FPdc; repeat from ★ across to last dc, dc in last dc: 4{5-6-7}{7-8-9} Shells and 2 dc.

Sizes Extra Small & Small ONLY

Row 3: Ch 3, turn; work FPdc around next BPdc, ★ work Shell in next ch-1 sp, work FPdc around next BPdc; repeat from ★ across to last dc, dc in last dc.

Row 4: Ch 3, turn; work BPdc around next FPdc, ★ work Shell in next ch-1 sp, work BPdc around next FPdc; repeat from ★ across to last dc, dc in last dc.

Rows 5-8: Repeat Rows 3 and 4 twice.

Sizes Medium, Large, Extra Large, 2X-Large, & 3X-Large ONLY

Row 3: Ch 3, turn; work FPdc around next BPdc, ★ work Shell in next ch-1 sp, work FPdc around next BPdc; repeat from ★ {4-5}{5-6-6} times **more**, dc in next 2 dc and in next ch-1 sp, leave remaining sts unworked: {5-6}{6-7-7} Shells and 4 dc.

Row 4: Turn; slip st in first 3 sts, ch 3, work BPdc around next FPdc, ★ work Shell in next ch-1 sp, work BPdc around next FPdc; repeat from ★ across to last dc, dc in last dc: {5-6}{6-7-7} Shells and 2 dc.

Row 5: Ch 3, turn; work FPdc around next BPdc, ★ work Shell in next ch-1 sp, work FPdc around next BPdc; repeat from ★ across to last dc, dc in last dc.

Row 6: Ch 3, turn; work BPdc around next FPdc, ★ work Shell in next ch-1 sp, work BPdc around next FPdc; repeat from ★ across to last dc, dc in last dc.

Rows 7-10: Repeat Rows 5 and 6 twice.

NECK SHAPING
All Sizes

Row 1: Turn; working in sts and in chs, slip st in first 5 sts, ch 2, dc in next 2 dc, work FPdc around next BPdc, ★ work Shell in next ch-1 sp, work FPdc around next BPdc; repeat from ★ across to last dc, dc in last dc: 3{4-4-5}{5-6-6} Shells.

Row 2: Ch 3, turn; work BPdc around next FPdc, ★ work Shell in next ch-1 sp, work BPdc around next FPdc; repeat from ★ across to last 3 sts, dc in next dc, leave remaining sts unworked.

Rows 3 and 4: Repeat Rows 1 and 2: 2{3-3-4}{4-5-5} Shells.

Size Extra Small ONLY
Row 5: Turn; working in sts and in chs, slip st in first 5 sts, ch 2, dc in next 2 dc, work FPdc around next BPdc, work Shell in next ch-1 sp, work FPdc around next BPdc, dc in last dc: one Shell.

Row 6: Ch 3, turn; work BPdc around next FPdc, work Shell in next ch-1 sp, work BPdc around next FPdc, dc in last 3 sts.

Row 7: Ch 3, turn; dc in next 2 dc, work FPdc around next BPdc, work Shell in next ch-1 sp, work FPdc around next BPdc, dc in last dc.

Row 8: Repeat Row 6; finish off.

Sizes Small, Medium, Large, Extra Large, 2X-Large, & 3X-Large ONLY
Row 5: Turn; working in sts and in chs, slip st in first 5 sts, ch 2, dc in next 2 dc, work FPdc around next BPdc, ★ work Shell in next ch-1 sp, work FPdc around next BPdc; repeat from ★ across to last dc, dc in last dc: {2-2-3}{3-4-4} Shells.

Row 6: Ch 3, turn; work BPdc around next FPdc, ★ work Shell in next ch-1 sp, work BPdc around next FPdc; repeat from ★ across to last 3 sts, dc in next dc, leave remaining sts unworked.

Instructions continued on page 92.

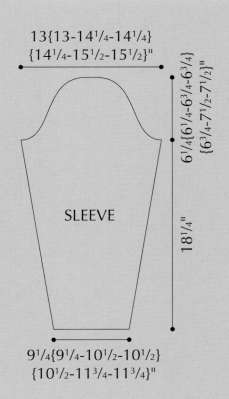

13{13-14$\frac{1}{4}$-14$\frac{1}{4}$}
{14$\frac{1}{4}$-15$\frac{1}{2}$-15$\frac{1}{2}$}"

6$\frac{1}{4}${6$\frac{1}{4}$-6$\frac{3}{4}$-6$\frac{3}{4}$}
{6$\frac{3}{4}$-7$\frac{1}{2}$-7$\frac{1}{2}$}"

SLEEVE

18$\frac{1}{4}$"

9$\frac{1}{4}${9$\frac{1}{4}$-10$\frac{1}{2}$-10$\frac{1}{2}$}
{10$\frac{1}{2}$-11$\frac{3}{4}$-11$\frac{3}{4}$}"

Sizes Small, Medium, Large, & Extra Large ONLY
Row 7: Ch 3, turn; work FPdc around next BPdc, ★ work Shell in next ch-1 sp, work FPdc around next BPdc; repeat from ★ across to last dc, dc in last dc.

Sizes Medium & Large ONLY
Finish off.

Sizes Small & Extra Large ONLY
Row 8: Ch 3, turn; work BPdc around next FPdc, ★ work Shell in next ch-1 sp, work BPdc around next FPdc; repeat from ★ across to last dc, dc in last dc; finish off.

Sizes 2X-Large & 3X-Large ONLY
Row 7: Turn; working in sts and in chs, slip st in first 5 sts, ch 2, dc in next 2 dc, work FPdc around next BPdc, ★ work Shell in next ch-1 sp, work FPdc around next BPdc; repeat from ★ across to last dc, dc in last dc: 3 Shells.

Row 8: Ch 3, turn; work BPdc around next FPdc, ★ work Shell in next ch-1 sp, work BPdc around next FPdc; repeat from ★ across to last 3 sts, dc in next dc, leave remaining sts unworked.

Size 2X-Large ONLY
Finish off.

Size 3X ONLY
Row 9: Ch 3, turn; work FPdc around next BPdc, ★ work Shell in next ch-1 sp, work FPdc around next BPdc; repeat from ★ across to last dc, dc in last dc; finish off.

SLEEVE (Make 2)
With larger size hook,
ch 46{46-52-52}{52-58-58}.

Row 1 (Right side)**:** Sc in second ch from hook and in each ch across: 45{45-51-51}{51-57-57} sc.

Note: Mark Row 1 as **right** side.

Row 2: Ch 3, turn; dc in next sc, skip next 2 sc, work Shell in next sc, ★ skip next 2 sc, dc in next sc, skip next 2 sc, work Shell in next sc; repeat from ★ across to last 4 sc, skip next 2 sc, dc in last 2 sc: 7{7-8-8}{8-9-9} Shells.

Row 3: Ch 3, turn; work FPdc around next dc, ★ work Shell in next ch-1 sp, skip next 2 dc, work FPdc around next dc; repeat from ★ across to last dc, dc in last dc: 7{7-8-8}{8-9-9} Shells and 2 dc.

Row 4: Ch 3, turn; work BPdc around next FPdc, ★ work Shell in next ch-1 sp, work BPdc around next FPdc; repeat from ★ across to last dc, dc in last dc.

Row 5 (Increase row)**:** Ch 3, turn; dc in same st, work FPdc around next BPdc, ★ work Shell in next ch-1 sp, work FPdc around next BPdc; repeat from ★ across to last dc, 2 dc in last dc: 7{7-8-8}{8-9-9} Shells and 4 dc.

Row 6: Ch 3, turn; dc in next dc, work BPdc around next FPdc, ★ work Shell in next ch-1 sp, work BPdc around next FPdc; repeat from ★ across to last 2 dc, dc in last 2 dc.

Row 7: Ch 3, turn; dc in next dc, work FPdc around next BPdc, ★ work Shell in next ch-1 sp, work FPdc around next BPdc; repeat from ★ across to last 2 dc, dc in last 2 dc.

Row 8: Repeat Row 6.

Row 9 (Increase row)**:** Ch 3, turn; dc in same st and in next dc, work FPdc around next BPdc, ★ work Shell in next ch-1 sp, work FPdc around next BPdc; repeat from ★ across to last 2 dc, dc in next dc, 2 dc in last dc: 7{7-8-8}{8-9-9} Shells and 6 dc.

Row 10: Ch 3, turn; dc in next 2 dc, work BPdc around next FPdc, ★ work Shell in next ch-1 sp, work BPdc around next FPdc; repeat from ★ across to last 3 dc, dc in last 3 dc.

Row 11: Ch 3, turn; dc in next 2 dc, work FPdc around next BPdc, ★ work Shell in next ch-1 sp, work FPdc around next BPdc; repeat from ★ across to last 3 dc, dc in last 3 dc.

Row 12: Repeat Row 10.

Row 13 (Increase row)**:** Ch 3, turn; dc in same st and in next 2 dc, work FPdc around next BPdc, ★ work Shell in next ch-1 sp, work FPdc around next BPdc; repeat from ★ across to last 3 dc, dc in next 2 dc, 2 dc in last dc: 7{7-8-8}{8-9-9} Shells and 8 dc.

Row 14: Ch 3, turn; dc in next 3 dc, work BPdc around next FPdc, ★ work Shell in next ch-1 sp, work BPdc around next FPdc; repeat from ★ across to last 4 dc, dc in last 4 dc.

Row 15: Ch 3, turn; dc in next 3 dc, work FPdc around next BPdc, ★ work Shell in next ch-1 sp, work FPdc around next BPdc; repeat from ★ across to last 4 dc, dc in last 4 dc.

Row 16: Repeat Row 14.

Row 17 (Increase row)**:** Ch 3, turn; dc in same st, skip next dc, work Shell in next dc, skip next dc, work FPdc around next BPdc, ★ work Shell in next ch-1 sp, work FPdc around next BPdc; repeat from ★ across to last 4 dc, skip next dc, work Shell in next dc, skip next dc, 2 dc in last dc: 9{9-10-10}{10-11-11} Shells and 4 dc.

Row 18: Ch 3, turn; work BPdc around next dc, work Shell in next ch-1 sp, ★ work BPdc around next FPdc, work Shell in next ch-1 sp; repeat from ★ across to last 4 dc, skip next 2 dc, work BPdc around next dc, dc in last dc: 9{9-10-10}{10-11-11} Shells and 2 dc.

Row 19: Ch 3, turn; work FPdc around next BPdc, ★ work Shell in next ch-1 sp, work FPdc around next BPdc; repeat from ★ across to last dc, dc in last dc.

Rows 20-32: Repeat Rows 4-16: 9{9-10-10} {10-11-11} Shells and 8 dc.

CAP SHAPING

Row 1: Turn; slip st in first 5 sts, ch 3, work Shell in next ch-1 sp, ★ work FPdc around next BPdc, work Shell in next ch-1 sp; repeat from ★ across to last 7 sts, skip next 2 dc, dc in next BPdc, leave remaining dc unworked: 9{9-10-10} {10-11-11} Shells and 2 dc.

Row 2: Turn; slip st in first 3 dc and in next ch-1 sp, ch 3, work BPdc around next FPdc, ★ work Shell in next ch-1 sp, work BPdc around next FPdc; repeat from ★ across to last ch-1 sp, dc in last ch-1 sp, leave remaining sts unworked: 7{7-8-8}{8-9-9} Shells and 2 dc.

Row 3: Ch 3, turn; work FPdc around next BPdc, ★ work Shell in next ch-1 sp, work FPdc around next BPdc; repeat from ★ across to last dc, dc in last dc.

Row 4: Ch 3, turn; work BPdc around next FPdc, ★ work Shell in next ch-1 sp, work BPdc around next FPdc; repeat from ★ across to last dc, dc in last dc.

Row 5: Ch 3, turn; work FPdc around next BPdc, ★ work Shell in next ch-1 sp, work FPdc around next BPdc; repeat from ★ across to last dc, leave last dc unworked: 7{7-8-8}{8-9-9} Shells and one dc.

Row 6: Turn; slip st in first 3 sts and in next ch-1 sp, ch 3, dc in next 2 dc, ★ work BPdc around next FPdc, work Shell in next ch-1 sp; repeat from ★ across to last FPdc, work BPdc around next FPdc, dc in next 2 dc and in last ch-1 sp, leave remaining sts unworked: 5{5-6-6}{6-7-7} Shells and 6 dc.

Row 7: Turn; slip st in first 2 dc, ch 2, dc in next dc, work FPdc around next BPdc, ★ work Shell in next ch-1 sp, work FPdc around next BPdc; repeat from ★ across to last 3 dc, dc in next dc, hdc in next dc, leave remaining dc unworked.

Instructions continued on page 94.

Row 8: Turn; slip st in first 3 sts, ch 2, work Shell in next ch-1 sp, ★ work BPdc around next FPdc, work Shell in next ch-1 sp; repeat from ★ across to last 5 sts, skip next 2 dc, hdc in next FPdc, leave remaining sts unworked: 5{5-6-6}{6-7-7} Shells.

Row 9: Turn; slip st in first 3 sts and in next ch-1 sp, ch 3, dc in next 2 dc, ★ work FPdc around next BPdc, work Shell in next ch-1 sp; repeat from ★ across to last BPdc, work FPdc around next BPdc, dc in next 2 dc and in last ch-1 sp, leave remaining sts unworked: 3{3-4-4}{4-5-5} Shells and 6 dc.

Row 10: Turn; slip st in first 3 dc, ch 3, work BPdc around next FPdc, ★ work Shell in next ch-1 sp, work BPdc around next FPdc; repeat from ★ across to last 3 dc, dc in next dc, leave remaining sts unworked: 3{3-4-4}{4-5-5} Shells and 2 dc.

Sizes Extra Small, Small, Medium, Large, & Extra Large ONLY
Row 11: Turn; slip st in first 2 sts, ch 2, work Shell in next ch-1 sp, ★ work FPdc around next BPdc, work Shell in next ch-1 sp; repeat from ★ across to last 4 sts, skip next 2 dc, hdc in next BPdc, leave remaining st unworked: 3{3-4-4}{4} Shells.

Size Extra Small & Small ONLY
Finish off.

Sizes Medium, Large, & Extra Large ONLY
Row 12: Ch 2, turn; work Shell in next ch-1 sp, ★ work BPdc around next FPdc, work Shell in next ch-1 sp; repeat from ★ across to last 3 sts, skip next 2 dc, hdc in last st; finish off.

Sizes 2X-Large & 3X-Large ONLY
Row 11: Ch 2, turn; work FPdc around next BPdc, ★ work Shell in next ch-1 sp, work FPdc around next BPdc; repeat from ★ across to last dc, leave remaining dc unworked: 5 Shells.

Row 12: Turn; slip st in first 3 sts and in next ch-1 sp, ch 3, dc in next 2 dc, ★ work BPdc around next FPdc, work Shell in next ch-1 sp; repeat from ★ across to last FPdc, work BPdc around next FPdc, dc in next 2 dc and in last ch-1 sp, leave remaining sts unworked: 3 Shells and 6 dc.

Row 13: Turn; slip st in first 2 sts, ch 3, dc in next dc, work FPdc around next BPdc, ★ work Shell in next ch-1 sp, work FPdc around next BPdc; repeat from ★ across to last 3 dc, dc in next 2 dc, leave remaining dc unworked; finish off: 3 Shells and 4 dc.

FINISHING
Whipstitch shoulder seams **(Fig. 7, page 127)**.

Weave Sleeves to Sweater **(Fig. 6, page 127)**.

Weave underarm and side in one continuous seam.

BOTTOM RIBBING
With smaller size hook, ch 16.

Row 1 (Right side)**:** Sc in second ch from hook and in each ch across: 15 sc.

Change to larger size hook.

Row 2: Ch 1, turn; slip st in Front Loop Only of each st across **(Fig. 1, page 125)**.

Repeat Row 2 until Ribbing measures approximately 26^1/$_2${31^1/$_2$-36^1/$_2$-41^1/$_2$}{46^1/$_2$-51^1/$_2$-56^1/$_2$}"/67.5{80-92.5-105.5}{118-131-143.5} cm.

Finish off.

Fold Ribbing in half with **right** sides facing. Pin fold to center back, then gently stretch Ribbing to meet at front edges, securing with pins.

Whipstitch Ribbing to bottom edge.

NECK RIBBING

With smaller size hook, ch 9.

Row 1 (Right side)**:** Sc in second ch from hook and in each ch across: 8 sc.

Change to larger size hook.

Row 2: Ch 1, turn; slip st in Front Loop Only of each st across.

Repeat Row 2 until Ribbing measures approximately 17{17½-18-18½}{19-19½-20}"/ 43{44.5-45.5-47}{48.5-49.5-51} cm.

Finish off.

Fold Ribbing in half with **right** sides facing. Pin fold to neck at center back, then gently stretch Ribbing to meet at front edges, securing with pins.

Whipstitch Ribbing to neck edge.

RIGHT FRONT RIBBING

With smaller size hook, ch 18.

Row 1 (Right side)**:** Sc in second ch from hook and in each ch across: 17 sc.

Change to larger size hook.

Rows 2 thru 5{5-5-7}{7-7-7}: Ch 1, turn; slip st in Front Loop Only of each st across.

Row 6{6-6-8}{8-8-8} (Buttonhole row)**:** Ch 1, turn; working in Front Loops Only, slip st in first 3 sts, ch 3, skip next 2 sts (buttonhole), slip st in next 7 sts, ch 3, skip next 2 sts (buttonhole), slip st in last 3 sts.

Row 7{7-7-9}{9-9-9}: Ch 1, turn; slip st in Front Loop Only of each st across to next ch-3, slip st in next ch, skip next ch, slip st in next ch and in Front Loop Only of each st across to next ch-3, slip st in next ch, skip next ch, slip st in next ch and in Front Loop Only of each st across.

Next 14{14-14-16}{16-16-16} Rows: Ch 1, turn; slip st in Front Loop Only of each st across.

Repeat last 16{16-16-18}{18-18-18} rows, 3 times **more**.

Buttonhole Row: Ch 1, turn; working in Front Loops Only, slip st in first 3 sts, ch 3, skip next 2 sts (buttonhole), slip st in next 7 sts, ch 3, skip next 2 sts (buttonhole), slip st in last 3 sts.

Next Row: Ch 1, turn; slip st in Front Loop Only of each st across to next ch-3, slip st in next ch, skip next ch, slip st in next ch and in Front Loop Only of each st across to next ch-3, slip st in next ch, skip next ch, slip st in next ch and in Front Loop Only of each st across.

Last 8{8-10-10}{12-12-12} Rows: Ch 1, turn; slip st in Front Loop Only of each st across.

Finish off.

LEFT FRONT RIBBING

Work same as Right Front Ribbing, eliminating buttonholes.

With **right** side of Ribbing and corresponding Front facing, gently stretch Ribbing piece to match Front and pin in place; then whipstitch together.

Sew buttons to Left Front opposite buttonholes.

Nice Striped Vest

◼◼◼◻ **INTERMEDIATE**

Size	Finished Chest Measurement
Extra Small	30" (76 cm)
Small	34" (86.5 cm)
Medium	38" (96.5 cm)
Large	42" (106.5 cm)
Extra Large	46" (117 cm)
2X-Large	50" (127 cm)
3X-Large	54" (137 cm)

Size Note: Instructions are written for size Extra Small with sizes Small, Medium, and Large in first set of braces { } and sizes Extra Large, 2X-Large, and 3X-Large in second set of braces. Instructions will be easier to read if you circle all the numbers pertaining to your size. If only one number is given, it applies to all sizes.

MATERIALS

Light Weight Yarn
[3 ounces, 251 yards
(85 grams, 230 meters) per skein]:
   MC (Blue) - 3{3-3-4}{4-5-5} skeins
   CC (Green) - 2{2-3-3}{4-4-4}) skeins
Crochet hook, size G (4 mm) **or** size needed for gauge
Yarn needle
Sewing needle and thread
1¹⁄₈" (29 mm) Buttons - 5

GAUGE: 20 sc and 22 rows = 4" (10 cm)
In pattern, (work Cluster, ch 1) 10 times and 16 rows = 4" (10 cm)

Gauge Swatches
4" (10 cm) square
With MC, ch 21.
Row 1: Sc in second ch from hook and in each ch across: 20 sc.
Rows 2-22: Ch 1, turn; sc in each sc across.
Finish off.

4¹⁄₈" (10.5 cm) square
With CC, ch 24.
Row 1 (Right side)**:** Sc in second ch from hook and in each ch across: 23 sc.
Rows 2-17: Beginning with Row 5, work same as Back, page 98, for 16 rows.
Finish off.

Instructions continued on page 98.

Vest

STITCH GUIDE

CLUSTER (uses next 2 sps)
YO, working around previous row, insert hook in **same** sp as last Cluster or dc worked 2 rows **below**, YO and pull up a loop, YO and draw through 2 loops on hook, YO, insert hook in next ch-1 sp 2 rows **below**, YO and pull up a loop, YO and draw through 2 loops on hook, YO and draw through all 3 loops on hook.

ENDING CLUSTER (uses one sp and one sc)
YO, working around previous row, insert hook in **same** sp as last Cluster worked 2 rows **below**, YO and pull up a loop, YO and draw through 2 loops on hook, YO, insert hook in next sc, YO and pull up a loop, YO and draw through all 4 loops on hook.

BACK

With MC, ch 76{86-96-106}{116-126-136}.

Row 1 (Right side)**:** Sc in second ch from hook and in each ch across: 75{85-95-105}{115-125-135} sc.

Note: Loop a short piece of yarn around any stitch to mark Row 1 as **right** side.

Rows 2 and 3: Ch 1, turn; sc in each sc across.

Row 4: Ch 1, turn; sc in each sc across changing to CC in last sc *(Fig. 3, page 126)*.

Carry unused color along side of piece.

Row 5: Ch 3 **(counts as first dc)**, turn; dc in next sc, ch 1, ★ [YO, insert hook in **same** sc as last st worked, YO and pull up a loop, YO and draw through 2 loops on hook, YO, skip next sc, insert hook in **next** sc, YO and pull up a loop,

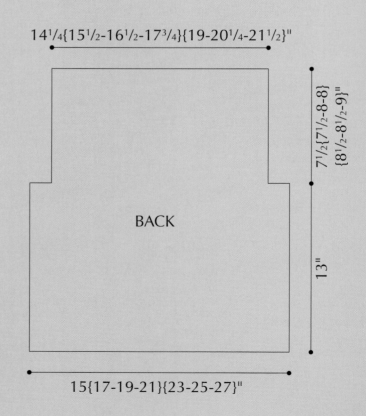

14¼{15½-16½-17¾}{19-20¼-21½}"

7½{7½-8-8}{8½-8½-9}"

13"

BACK

15{17-19-21}{23-25-27}"

YO and draw through 2 loops on hook, YO and draw through all 3 loops on hook (**counts as one Cluster)**], ch 1; repeat from ★ across to last sc, [YO, insert hook in **same** sc as last st worked, YO and pull up a loop, YO and draw through 2 loops on hook, YO, insert hook in last sc, YO and pull up a loop, YO and draw through 2 loops on hook, YO and draw through all 3 loops on hook (**counts as one Cluster)**]: 39{44-49-54}{59-64-69} sts and 37{42-47-52}{57-62-67} ch-1 sps.

Row 6: Ch 1, turn; sc in first st, ch 1, ★ skip next ch-1 sp, sc in next st, ch 1; repeat from ★ across to last ch-1 sp, skip last ch-1 sp and next dc, sc in last dc changing to MC: 38{43-48-53}{58-63-68} sc and 37{42-47-52}{57-62-67} ch-1 sps.

Row 7: Ch 2 (**counts as first hdc, now and throughout**), turn; working around previous row, dc in next ch-1 sp 2 rows **below**, ch 1, (work Cluster, ch 1) across to last sc, work Ending Cluster: 39{44-49-54}{59-64-69} sts and 37{42-47-52}{57-62-67} ch-1 sps.

Row 8: Ch 1, turn; sc in first st, ch 1, ★ skip next ch-1 sp, sc in next st, ch 1; repeat from ★ across to last ch-1 sp, skip last ch-1 sp and next dc, sc in last hdc changing to CC: 38{43-48-53}{58-63-68} sc and 37{42-47-52}{57-62-67} ch-1 sps.

Row 9: Ch 2, turn; dc in next ch-1 sp 2 rows **below**, ch 1, (work Cluster, ch 1) across to last sc, work Ending Cluster: 39{44-49-54}{59-64-69} sts and 37{42-47-52}{57-62-67} ch-1 sps.

Row 10: Ch 1, turn; sc in first st, ch 1, ★ skip next ch-1 sp, sc in next st, ch 1; repeat from ★ across to last ch-1 sp, skip last ch-1 sp and next dc, sc in last hdc changing to MC: 38{43-48-53}{58-63-68} sc and 37{42-47-52}{57-62-67} ch-1 sps.

Repeat Rows 7-10 for pattern until piece measures approximately 13" (33 cm) from beginning ch, ending by working Row 8.

ARMHOLE SHAPING

Row 1: Turn; working in sc and in chs, slip st in first 3{5-7-9}{11-13-15} sts, ch 2, dc in next ch-1 sp 2 rows **below**, ch 1, (work Cluster, ch 1) across to last 1{2-3-4}{5-6-7} ch-1 sp(s), work Ending Cluster, leave remaining sts unworked: 37{40-43-46}{49-52-55} sts and 35{38-41-44}{47-50-53} ch-1 sps.

Row 2: Ch 1, turn; sc in first st, ch 1, ★ skip next ch-1 sp, sc in next st, ch 1; repeat from ★ across to last ch-1 sp, skip last ch-1 sp and next dc, sc in last hdc changing to MC: 36{39-42-45}{48-51-54} sc and 35{38-41-44}{47-50-53} ch-1 sps.

Row 3: Ch 2, turn; dc in next ch-1 sp 2 rows **below**, ch 1, (work Cluster, ch 1) across to last sc, work Ending Cluster: 37{40-43-46}{49-52-55} sts and 35{38-41-44}{47-50-53} ch-1 sps.

Row 4: Ch 1, turn; sc in first st, ch 1, ★ skip next ch-1 sp, sc in next st, ch 1; repeat from ★ across to last ch-1 sp, skip last ch-1 sp and next dc, sc in last hdc changing to CC: 36{39-42-45}{48-51-54} sc and 35{38-41-44}{47-50-53} ch-1 sps.

Row 5: Ch 2, turn; dc in next ch-1 sp 2 rows **below**, ch 1, (work Cluster, ch 1) across to last sc, work Ending Cluster: 37{40-43-46}{49-52-55} sts and 35{38-41-44}{47-50-53} ch-1 sps.

Row 6: Ch 1, turn; sc in first st, ch 1, ★ skip next ch-1 sp, sc in next st, ch 1; repeat from ★ across to last ch-1 sp, skip last ch-1 sp and next dc, sc in last hdc changing to MC: 36{39-42-45}{48-51-54} sc and 35{38-41-44}{47-50-53} ch-1 sps.

Rows 7 thru 30{30-32-32}{34-34-36}: Repeat Rows 3-6, 6{6-6-6}{7-7-7} times; then repeat Rows 3 and 4, 0{0-1-1}{0-0-1} time(s) **more (see Zeros, page 125)**; do **not** change color at end of last row.

Finish off.

Instructions continued on page 100.

LEFT FRONT

With MC, ch 40{46-50-56}{60-66-70}.

Work same as Back, page 98, to Armhole Shaping: 20{23-25-28}{30-33-35} sc and 19{22-24-27}{29-32-34} ch-1 sps.

ARMHOLE AND NECK SHAPING

Row 1: Turn; working in sc and in chs, slip st in first 3{5-7-9}{11-13-15} sts, ch 2, dc in next ch-1 sp 2 rows **below**, ch 1, (work Cluster, ch 1) across to last sc, work Ending Cluster: 20{22-23-25}{26-28-29} sts and 18{20-21-23}{24-26-27} ch-1 sps.

Place marker in end of last row for Edging.

Row 2 (Decrease row)**:** Turn; slip st in first st and in next ch-1 sp, ch 1, sc in next st, ch 1, ★ skip next ch-1 sp, sc in next st, ch 1; repeat from ★ across to last ch-1 sp, skip last ch-1 sp and next dc, sc in last hdc changing to MC: 18{20-21-23}{24-26-27} sc and 17{19-20-22}{23-25-26} ch-1 sps.

Row 3: Ch 2, turn; dc in next ch-1 sp 2 rows **below**, ch 1, (work Cluster, ch 1) across to last sc, work Ending Cluster, leave last 2 slip sts unworked: 19{21-22-24}{25-27-28} sts and 17{19-20-22}{23-25-26} ch-1 sps.

Row 4 (Decrease row)**:** Turn; slip st in first st and in next ch-1 sp, ch 1, sc in next st, ch 1, ★ skip next ch-1 sp, sc in next st, ch 1; repeat from ★ across to last ch-1 sp, skip last ch-1 sp and next dc, sc in last hdc changing to CC: 17{19-20-22}{23-25-26} sc and 16{18-19-21}{22-24-25} ch-1 sps.

Row 5: Ch 2, turn; dc in next ch-1 sp 2 rows **below**, ch 1, (work Cluster, ch 1) across to last sc, work Ending Cluster, leave last 2 slip sts unworked: 18{20-21-23}{24-26-27} sts and 16{18-19-21}{22-24-25} ch-1 sps.

Rows 6 thru 27{27-29-29}{31-31-33}: Repeat Rows 2-5, 5{5-6-6}{6-6-7} times; then repeat Rows 2 and 3, 1{1-0-0}{1-1-0} time(s) **more**: 7{9-9-11}{11-13-13} sts and 5{7-7-9}{9-11-11} ch-1 sps.

Row 28{28-30-30}{32-32-34}: Ch 1, turn; sc in first st, ch 1, ★ skip next ch-1 sp, sc in next st, ch 1; repeat from ★ across to last ch-1 sp, skip last ch-1 sp and next dc, sc in last hdc changing to next color in stripe sequence: 6{8-8-10}{10-12-12} sc and 5{7-7-9}{9-11-11} ch-1 sps.

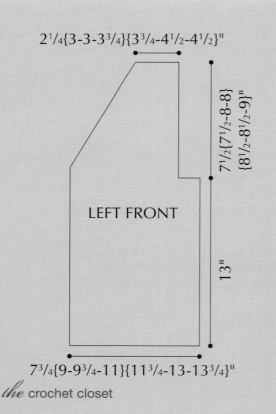

2¼{3-3-3¾}{3¾-4½-4½}"

7½{7½-8-8}{8½-8½-9}"

13"

LEFT FRONT

7¾{9-9¾-11}{11¾-13-13¾}"

Row 29{29-31-31}{33-33-35}: Ch 2, turn; dc in next ch-1 sp 2 rows **below**, ch 1, (work Cluster, ch 1) across to last sc, work Ending Cluster: 7{9-9-11}{11-13-13} sts and 5{7-7-9}{7-11-11} ch-1 sps.

Row 30{30-32-32}{34-34-36}: Ch 1, turn; sc in first st, ch 1, ★ skip next ch-1 sp, sc in next st, ch 1; repeat from ★ across to last ch-1 sp, skip last ch-1 sp and next dc, sc in last hdc; finish off: 6{8-8-10}{10-12-12} sc and 5{7-7-9}{9-11-11} ch-1 sps.

RIGHT FRONT

With MC, ch 40{46-50-56}{60-66-70}.

Work same as Back, page 98, to Armhole Shaping: 20{23-25-28}{30-33-35} sc and 19{22-24-27}{29-32-34} ch-1 sps.

ARMHOLE AND NECK SHAPING

Row 1: Ch 2, turn; dc in next ch-1 sp 2 rows **below**, ch 1, (work Cluster, ch 1) across to last 1{2-3-4}{5-6-7} ch-1 sp(s), work Ending Cluster, leave remaining sts unworked: 20{22-23-25}{26-28-29} sts and 18{20-21-23}{24-26-27} ch-1 sps.

Place marker in beginning of last row for Edging.

Row 2 (Decrease row): Ch 1, turn; sc in first st, ch 1, ★ skip next ch-1 sp, sc in next st, ch 1; repeat from ★ across to last 2 ch-1 sps, skip next ch-1 sp, sc in next st changing to MC, leave remaining sts unworked: 18{20-21-23}{24-26-27} sc and 17{19-20-22}{23-25-26} ch-1 sps.

Row 3: Ch 2, turn; dc in next ch-1 sp 2 rows **below**, ch 1, (work Cluster, ch 1) across to last sc, work Ending Cluster: 19{21-22-24}{25-27-28} sts and 17{19-20-22}{23-25-26} ch-1 sps.

Row 4 (Decrease row): Ch 1, turn; sc in first st, ch 1, ★ skip next ch-1 sp, sc in next st, ch 1; repeat from ★ across to last 2 ch-1 sps, skip next ch-1 sp, sc in next dc changing to CC, leave remaining sts unworked: 17{19-20-22}{23-25-26} sc and 16{18-19-21}{22-24-25} ch-1 sps.

Row 5: Ch 2, turn; dc in next ch-1 sp 2 rows **below**, ch 1, (work Cluster, ch 1) across to last sc, work Ending Cluster: 18{20-21-23}{24-26-27} sts and 16{18-19-21}{22-24-25} ch-1 sps.

Rows 6 thru 27{27-29-29}{31-31-33}: Repeat Rows 2-5, 5{5-6-6}{6-6-7} times; then repeat Rows 2 and 3, 1{1-0-0}{1-1-0} time(s) **more**: 7{9-9-11}{11-13-13} sts and 5{7-7-9}{9-11-11} ch-1 sps.

Complete same as Left Front.

FINISHING

Whipstitch shoulder seams *(Fig. 7, page 127)*.

Weave side seams *(Fig. 6, page 127)*.

ARMHOLE EDGING

Rnd 1: With **right** side facing, join MC with sc in side seam; *(see Joining With Sc, page 125)*; sc evenly around armhole; join with slip st to first sc.

Rnds 2-5: Ch 1, turn; sc in each sc around; join with slip st to first sc; at end of Rnd 5, finish off.

NECK EDGING

Row 1: With **right** side facing, join MC with sc in bottom corner of Right Front; working in end of rows, work 64 sc evenly spaced across to next marker, 3 sc in marked row, sc evenly across to next marker, 3 sc in marked row, work 65 sc evenly spaced across to bottom corner of Left Front.

Row 2: Ch 1, turn; sc in each sc across.

Row 3: Ch 1, turn; sc in first 5 sc, ch 3, skip next 2 sc (buttonhole made), ★ sc in next 12 sc, ch 3, skip next 2 sc (buttonhole made); repeat from ★ 3 times **more**, sc in each sc across.

Row 4: Ch 1, turn; ★ sc in each sc across to next ch-3 sp, 2 sc in ch-3 sp; repeat from ★ 4 times **more**, sc in each sc across.

Row 5: Ch 1, turn; sc in each sc across; finish off.

Sew buttons to Left Front opposite buttonholes.

Elegant Swing Coat

◼◼◼▢ INTERMEDIATE

Size	Finished Chest Measurement
Extra Small	32$^1/_2$" (82.5 cm)
Small	35" (89 cm)
Medium	39$^1/_2$" (100.5 cm)
Large	42" (106.5 cm)
Extra Large	46$^1/_2$" (118 cm)
2X-Large	51" (129.5 cm)
3X-Large	55$^1/_2$" (141 cm)

Size Note: Instructions are written for size Extra Small, with sizes Small, Medium, and Large in first set of braces { } and sizes Extra Large, 2X-Large, and 3X-Large in second set of braces. Instructions will be easier to read if you circle all the numbers pertaining to your size. If only one number is given, it applies to all sizes.

MATERIALS

Medium Weight Yarn
  [3.5 ounces, 220 yards
  (100 grams, 201 meters) per hank]:
    10{10-11-11}{12-12-13} hanks
Crochet hook, size H (5 mm) **or** size needed for gauge
Yarn needle

GAUGE: In pattern, 21 sts (7 repeats) and 14 rows = 4" (10 cm)

Gauge Swatch: 4$^1/_2$" (11.5 cm) square
Ch 24.
Work same as Back, page 104, for 16 rows.
Finish off.

Instructions continued on page 104.

Coat

BACK

Ch 87{93-105-111}{123-135-147}.

Row 1 (Right side): Sc in second ch from hook and in each ch across: 86{92-104-110}{122-134-146} sc.

Note: Loop a short piece of yarn around any stitch to mark Row 1 as **right** side.

Row 2: Ch 1, turn; sc in each sc across.

Row 3: Ch 1, turn; sc in first sc, (sc, ch 1, dc) in next sc, ★ skip next 2 sc, (sc, ch 1, dc) in next sc; repeat from ★ across to last 3 sc, skip next 2 sc, sc in last sc: 28{30-34-36}{40-44-48} ch-1 sps.

Row 4: Ch 1, turn; sc in first sc, (sc, ch 1, dc) in next ch-1 sp and in each ch-1 sp across to last 2 sc, skip next sc, sc in last sc.

Repeat Row 4 for pattern until piece measures approximately 17¼" (44 cm) from beginning ch, ending by working a **wrong** side row.

ARMHOLE SHAPING

Row 1: Turn; working in sts and in ch-1 sps, slip st in first 6{6-9-9}{12-15-18} sts, ch 1, sc in same ch-1 sp, (sc, ch 1, dc) in each ch-1 sp across to last 2{2-3-3}{4-5-6} ch-1 sps, sc in next ch-1 sp, leave remaining sts unworked: 24{26-28-30}{32-34-36} ch-1 sps.

Row 2: Ch 1, turn; sc in first sc, (sc, ch 1, dc) in next ch-1 sp and in each ch-1 sp across to last 2 sc, skip next sc, sc in last sc.

Repeat Row 2 for pattern until armholes measure approximately 7½{7½-8½-8½}{8½-9½-9½}"/ 19{19-21.5-21.5}{21.5-24-24} cm, ending by working a **right** side row.

Finish off.

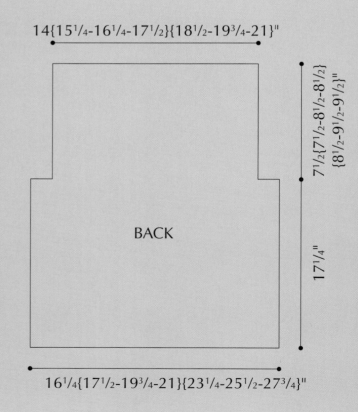

14{15¼-16¼-17½}{18½-19¾-21}"

7½{7½-8½-8½}{8½-9½-9½}"

BACK

17¼"

16¼{17½-19¾-21}{23¼-25½-27¾}"

LEFT FRONT

Ch 69{78-87-93}{99-105-111}.

Work same as Back to Armhole Shaping:
22{25-28-30}{32-34-36} ch-1 sps.

ARMHOLE SHAPING

Row 1: Turn; working in sts and in ch-1 sps, slip st
in first 6{6-9-9}{12-15-18} sts, ch 1, sc in same
ch-1 sp, (sc, ch 1, dc) in next ch-1 sp and in each
ch-1 sp across to last 2 sc, skip next sc, sc in last
sc: 20{23-25-27}{28-29-30} ch-1 sps.

Row 2: Ch 1, turn; sc in first sc, (sc, ch 1, dc)
in next ch-1 sp and in each ch-1 sp across to
last 2 sc, skip next sc, sc in last sc.

Repeat Row 2 until armhole measures same as
Back, ending by working a **right** side row.

Do **not** finish off.

COLLAR

Row 1: Ch 1, turn; sc in first sc, (sc, ch 1, dc) in
next ch-1 sp and in each ch-1 sp across to last
4{6-7-8}{8-9-9} ch-1 sps, sc in next ch-1 sp,
leave remaining sts unworked (shoulder):
16{17-18-19}{20-20-21} ch-1 sps.

Row 2: Ch 1, turn; sc in first sc, (sc, ch 1, dc) in
next ch-1 sp and in each ch-1 sp across to last
2 sc, skip next sc, sc in last sc.

Collar is worked in short rows, which achieves
more height at the neck edge than at the edge that
will be sewn to the Back neck edge.

Row 3 (Decrease row)**:** Ch 1, turn; sc in first sc,
(sc, ch 1, dc) in next ch-1 sp and in each ch-1 sp
across to last 2 ch-1 sps, slip st in next ch-1 sp,
leave remaining sts unworked:
14{15-16-17}{18-18-19} ch-1 sps.

Instructions continued on page 106.

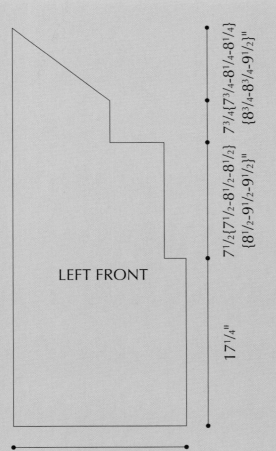

LEFT FRONT

7¹/₂{7¹/₂-8¹/₂-8¹/₂}{8¹/₂-9¹/₂-9¹/₂}"

7³/₄{7³/₄-8¹/₄-8¹/₄}{8³/₄-8³/₄-9¹/₂}"

17¹/₄"

13{14¹/₂-16¹/₄-17¹/₂}{18¹/₂-19³/₄-21}"

Row 4: Ch 1, turn; (sc, ch 1, dc) in next ch-1 sp and in each ch-1 sp across to last 2 sc, skip next sc, sc in last sc.

Row 5 (Increase row)**:** Ch 1, turn; sc in first sc, (sc, ch 1, dc) in next ch-1 sp and in each ch-1 sp across to unworked ch-1 sps 3 rows **below**, (sc, ch 1, dc) in each unworked ch-1 sp across, skip next sc, sc in last sc: 16{17-18-19}{20-20-21} ch-1 sps.

Row 6: Repeat Row 2.

Row 7 (Decrease row)**:** Ch 1, turn; sc in first sc, (sc, ch 1, dc) in next ch-1 sp and in each ch-1 sp across to last 3 ch-1 sps, slip st in next ch-1 sp, leave remaining sts unworked: 13{14-15-16}{17-17-18} ch-1 sps.

Rows 8 and 9: Repeat Rows 4 and 5.

Row 10: Repeat Row 2.

Row 11 (Decrease row)**:** Ch 1, turn; sc in first sc, (sc, ch 1, dc) in next ch-1 sp and in each ch-1 sp across to last 4 ch-1 sps, slip st in next ch-1 sp, leave remaining sts unworked: 12{13-14-15}{16-16-17} ch-1 sps.

Rows 12 and 13: Repeat Rows 4 and 5.

Rows 14-16: Repeat Row 2, 3 times.

Rows 17-27: Repeat Rows 3-13.

Sizes Medium and Large ONLY
Rows 28 and 29: Repeat Row 2 twice.

Sizes Extra Large and 2X-Large ONLY
Rows 28-31: Repeat Row 2, 4 times.

Sizes 3X-Large ONLY
Rows 28-33: Repeat Row 2, 6 times.

All Sizes
Finish off.

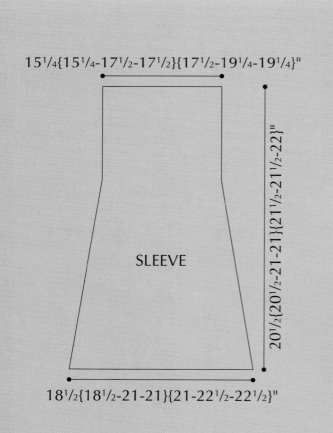

15¼{15¼-17½-17½}{17½-19¼-19¼}"

20½{20½-21-21}{21½-21½-22}"

SLEEVE

18½{18½-21-21}{21-22½-22½}"

RIGHT FRONT

Ch 69{78-87-93}{99-105-111}.

Work same as Back to Armhole Shaping: 22{25-28-30}{32-34-36} ch-1 sps.

ARMHOLE SHAPING

Row 1: Ch 1, turn; sc in first sc, (sc, ch 1, dc) in next ch-1 sp and in each ch-1 sp across to last 2{2-3-3}{4-5-6} ch-1 sps, sc in next ch-1 sp, leave remaining sts unworked: 20{23-25-27}{28-29-30} ch-1 sps.

Row 2: Ch 1, turn; sc in first sc, (sc, ch 1, dc) in next ch-1 sp and in each ch-1 sp across to last 2 sc, skip next sc, sc in last sc.

Repeat Row 2 until armhole measures same as Back, ending by working a **wrong** side row.

Do **not** finish off.

COLLAR
Work same as Left Front.

SLEEVE (Make 2)
Ch 99{99-111-111}{111-120-120}.

Row 1 (Right side): Sc in second ch from hook and in each ch across: 98{98-110-110}{110-119-119} sc.

Note: Mark Row 1 as **right** side.

Row 2: Ch 1, turn; sc in each sc across.

Row 3: Ch 1, turn; sc in first sc, ★ (sc, ch 1, dc) in next sc, skip next 2 sc; repeat from ★ across to last sc, sc in last sc: 32{32-36-36}{36-39-39} ch-1 sps.

Rows 4-10: Ch 1, turn; sc in first sc, (sc, ch 1, dc) in next ch-1 sp and in each ch-1 sp across to last 2 sc, skip next sc, sc in last sc.

Row 11 (Decrease row): Turn; slip st in first 2 sts and in next ch-1 sp, ch 1, sc in same sp, (sc, ch 1, dc) in next ch-1 sp and in each ch-1 sp across to last ch-1 sp, sc in last ch-1 sp, leave ramaining sc unworked: 30{30-34-34}{34-37-37} ch-1 sps.

Rows 12-22: Ch 1, turn; sc in first sc, (sc, ch 1, dc) in next ch-1 sp and in each ch-1 sp across to last 2 sc, skip next sc, sc in last sc.

Row 23: Repeat Row 11: 28{28-32-32}{32-35-35} ch-1 sps.

Rows 24-36: Ch 1, turn; sc in first sc, (sc, ch 1, dc) in next ch-1 sp and in each ch-1 sp across to last 2 sc, skip next sc, sc in last sc.

Row 37: Repeat Row 11: 26{26-30-30}{30-33-33} ch-1 sps.

Row 38: Ch 1, turn; sc in first sc, (sc, ch 1, dc) in next ch-1 sp and in each ch-1 sp across to last 2 sc, skip next sc, sc in last sc.

Repeat Row 38 until Sleeve measures approximately 20$\frac{1}{2}${20$\frac{1}{2}$-21-21}{21$\frac{1}{2}$-21$\frac{1}{2}$-22)"/ 52{52-53.5-53.5}{54.5-54.5-56} cm from beginning ch, ending by working a **wrong** side row.

Finish off.

FINISHING
Whipstitch shoulder seams (*Fig. 7, page 127*).

Whipstitch last row of each Collar together.

Whipstitch end of rows of inside edge of Collar to Back neck edge.

Weave Sleeves to Coat (*Fig. 6, page 127*).

Weave underarm and side in one continuous seam.

Sweater With Flair

◖■■■▭ INTERMEDIATE

Size	Finished Chest Measurement	
Extra Small	30½"	(77.5 cm)
Small	33"	(84 cm)
Medium	38"	(96.5 cm)
Large	43"	(109 cm)
Extra Large	48"	(122 cm)
2X-Large	53"	(134.5 cm)

Size Note: Instructions are written with sizes Extra Small, Small, and Medium in first set of braces { } and sizes Large, Extra Large, and 2X-Large in second set of braces. Instructions will be easier to read if you circle all the numbers pertaining to your size. If ONLY one number is given, it applies to all sizes.

MATERIALS

Light Weight Yarn
  [2.5 ounces, 168 yards
  (70 grams, 154 meters) per skein]:
    {10-10-11}{11-12-12} skeins
Crochet hook, size H (5 mm) **or** size needed
  for gauge
Yarn needle
Sewing needle and thread
⅞" (22 mm) Buttons - 3

GAUGE: 3 pattern repeats (18 sts) and
    12 rows = 3¾" (9.5 cm)

Gauge Swatch: 4" (10 cm) square
Ch 20.
Row 1 (Right side)**:** Sc in second ch from hook and in each ch across: 19 sc.
Row 2: Ch 1, turn; sc in each sc across.
Row 3: Ch 3 **(counts as first dc, now and throughout)**, turn; ★ skip next 2 sc, work Shell in next sc, skip next 2 sc, dc in next sc; repeat from ★ 2 times **more**.
Row 4: Ch 1, turn; sc in each dc and in each ch-1 sp across.
Rows 5-14: Repeat Rows 3 and 4, 5 times. Finish off.

Instructions continued on page 110.

STITCH GUIDE

SHELL
(2 Dc , ch 1, 2 dc) in st indicated.

BEGINNING SINGLE CROCHET DECREASE
   (abbreviated beginning sc decrease)
Pull up a loop in each of first 2 sts, YO and draw through all 3 loops on hook **(counts as one sc)**.

SINGLE CROCHET DECREASE
   (abbreviated sc decrease)
Pull up a loop in each of next 2 sts, YO and draw through all 3 loops on hook **(counts as one sc)**.

DOUBLE CROCHET DECREASE
   (abbreviated dc decrease) (uses next 2 sts)
★ YO, insert hook in **next** st, YO and pull up a loop, YO and draw through 2 loops on hook; repeat from ★ once **more**, YO and draw through all 3 loops on hook **(counts as one dc)**.

DOUBLE DECREASE (uses next 3 sts)
★ YO, insert hook in **next** st, YO and pull up a loop, YO and draw through 2 loops on hook; repeat from ★ 2 times **more**, YO and draw through all 4 loops **(counts as one dc)**.

BACK

Ch {94-100-112}{124-136-148}.

Row 1 (Right side)**:** Sc in second ch from hook and in each ch across: {93-99-111}{123-135-147} sc.

Note: Loop a short piece of yarn around any stitch to mark Row 1 as **right** side.

Row 2: Ch 1, turn; sc in each sc across.

Row 3: Ch 3 **(counts as first dc, now and throughout)**, turn; dc in next 4 sc, ★ † skip next 2 sc, work Shell in next sc, skip next 2 sc †, dc in next sc; repeat from ★ across to last 10 sc, then repeat from † to † once, dc in last 5 sc: {14-15-17}{19-21-23} Shells.

Row 4 AND ALL EVEN-NUMBERED ROWS: Ch 1, turn; sc in each dc and in each ch-1 sp across.

Row 5: Ch 3, turn; dc in next sc, ★ † skip next 2 sc, work Shell in next sc, skip next 2 sc †, dc in next sc; repeat from ★ across to last 7 sc, then repeat from † to † once, dc in last 2 sc: {15-16-18}{20-22-24} Shells.

Row 7: Ch 3, turn; dc decrease, dc in next 2 sc, ★ † skip next 2 sc, work Shell in next sc, skip next 2 sc †, dc in next sc; repeat from ★ across to last 10 sc, then repeat from † to † once, dc in next 2 sc, dc decrease, dc in last sc: {14-15-17}{19-21-23} Shells.

Row 9: Ch 3, turn; ★ skip next 2 sc, work Shell in next sc, skip next 2 sc, dc in next sc; repeat from ★ across: {15-16-18}{20-22-24} Shells.

Row 11: Ch 3, turn; dc decrease, dc in next sc, ★ skip next 2 sc, work Shell in next sc, skip next 2 sc, dc in next sc; repeat from ★ across to last 3 sc; dc decrease, dc in last sc: {14-15-17}{19-21-23} Shells.

Row 13: Ch 3, turn; dc decrease, dc in next 3 sc, ★ † skip next 2 sc, work Shell in next sc, skip next 2 sc †, dc in next sc; repeat from ★ across to last 11 sc, then repeat from † to † once, dc in next 3 sc, dc decrease, dc in last sc: {13-14-16}{18-20-22} Shells.

Row 15: Ch 3, turn; dc in next sc, ★ † skip next 2 sc, work Shell in next sc, skip next 2 sc †, dc in next sc; repeat from ★ across to last 7 sc, then repeat from † to † once, dc in last 2 sc: {14-15-17}{19-21-23} Shells.

Row 17: Ch 3, turn; dc decrease, dc in next 2 sc, ★ † skip next 2 sc, work Shell in next sc, skip next 2 sc †, dc in next sc; repeat from ★ across to last 10 sc, then repeat from † to † once, dc in next 2 sc, dc decrease, dc in last sc: {13-14-16}{18-20-22} Shells.

Row 19: Ch 3, turn; ★ skip next 2 sc, work Shell in next sc, skip next 2 sc, dc in next sc; repeat from ★ across: {14-15-17}{19-21-23} Shells.

Row 21: Ch 3, turn; dc in next 3 sc, ★ † skip next 2 sc, work Shell in next sc, skip next 2 sc †, dc in next sc; repeat from ★ across to last 9 sc, then repeat from † to † once, dc in last 4 sc: {13-14-16}{18-20-22} Shells.

Row 23: Ch 3, turn; dc decrease, dc in next 4 sc, ★ † skip next 2 sc, work Shell in next sc, skip next 2 sc †, dc in next sc; repeat from ★ across to last 12 sc, then repeat from † to † once, dc in next 4 sc, dc decrease, dc in last dc: {12-13-15}{17-19-21} Shells.

Row 25: Ch 3, turn; dc decrease, ★ † skip next 2 sc, work Shell in next sc, skip next 2 sc †, dc in next sc; repeat from ★ across to last 8 sc, then repeat from † to † once, dc decrease, dc in last dc: {13-14-16}{18-20-22} Shells.

Row 27: Ch 3, turn; dc in next 4 sc, ★ † skip next 2 sc, work Shell in next sc, skip next 2 sc †, dc in next sc; repeat from ★ across to last 10 sc, then repeat from † to † once, dc in last 5 sc: {12-13-15}{17-19-21} Shells.

Row 29: Ch 3, turn; dc in next sc, ★ † skip next 2 sc, work Shell in next sc, skip next 2 sc †, dc in next sc; repeat from ★ across to last 7 sc, then repeat from † to † once, dc in last 2 sc: {13-14-16}{18-20-22} Shells.

Row 31: Ch 3, turn; dc decrease, dc in next 2 sc, ★ † skip next 2 sc, work Shell in next sc, skip next 2 sc †, dc in next sc; repeat from ★ across to last 10 sc, then repeat from † to † once, dc in next 2 sc, dc decrease, dc in last sc: {12-13-15}{17-19-21} Shells.

Instructions continued on page 112.

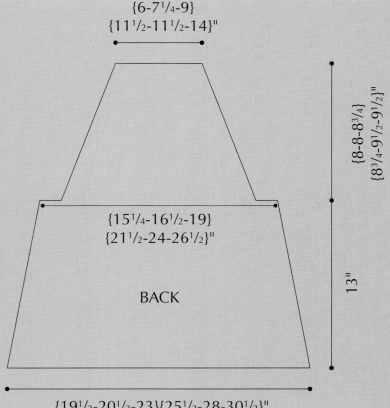

{6-7¹/₄-9}
{11¹/₂-11¹/₂-14}"

{8-8-8³/₄}
{8³/₄-9¹/₂-9¹/₂}"

{15¹/₄-16¹/₂-19}
{21¹/₂-24-26¹/₂}"

13"

BACK

{19¹/₂-20¹/₂-23}{25¹/₂-28-30¹/₂}"

Row 33: Ch 3, turn; dc decrease, dc in next 4 sc, ★ † skip next 2 sc, work Shell in next sc, skip next 2 sc †, dc in next sc; repeat from ★ across to last 12 sc, then repeat from † to † once, dc in next 4 sc, dc decrease, dc in last dc: {11-12-14}{16-18-20} Shells.

Row 35: Ch 3, turn; dc in next 2 sc, ★ † skip next 2 sc, work Shell in next sc, skip next 2 sc †, dc in next sc; repeat from ★ across to last 8 sc, then repeat from † to † once, dc in last 3 sc: {12-13-15}{17-19-21} Shells.

Row 37: Ch 3, turn; dc decrease, dc in next 3 sc, ★ † skip next 2 sc, work Shell in next sc, skip next 2 sc †, dc in next sc; repeat from ★ across to last 11 sc, then repeat from † to † once, dc in next 3 sc, dc decrease, dc in last dc: {11-12-14}{16-18-20} Shells.

Row 39: Ch 3, turn; dc in next sc, ★ † skip next 2 sc, work Shell in next sc, skip next 2 sc †, dc in next sc; repeat from ★ across to last 7 sc, then repeat from † to † once, dc in last 2 sc: {12-13-15}{17-19-21} Shells.

Row 41: Ch 3, turn; dc decrease, dc in next 2 sc, ★ † skip next 2 sc, work Shell in next sc, skip next 2 sc †, dc in next sc; repeat from ★ across to last 10 sc, then repeat from † to † once, dc in next 2 sc, dc decrease, dc in last sc: {11-12-14}{16-18-20} Shells.

Row 42: Ch 1, turn; sc in each dc and in each ch-1 sp across: {73-79-91}{103-115-127} sc.

RAGLAN ARMHOLE SHAPING

Row 1: Turn; slip st in first {6-6-6}{6-12-12} sc, ch 3, dc in next sc, ★ † skip next 2 sc, work Shell in next sc, skip next 2 sc †, dc in next sc; repeat from ★ {8-9-11}{13-13-15} times **more**, then repeat from † to † once, dc in next 2 sc, leave remaining sc unworked: {10-11-13}{15-15-17} Shells.

Row 2 AND ALL EVEN-NUMBERED ROWS: Ch 1, turn; sc in each dc and in each ch-1 sp across.

Row 3: Ch 3, turn; work double decrease, dc in next sc, ★ skip next 2 sc, work Shell in next sc, skip next 2 sc, dc in next sc; repeat from ★ across to last 4 sc, work double decrease, dc in last sc: {9-10-12}{14-14-16} Shells.

Row 5: Ch 3, turn; work double decrease, dc in next 2 sc, ★ † skip next 2 sc, work Shell in next sc, skip next 2 sc †, dc in next sc; repeat from ★ across to last 11 sc, then repeat from † to † once, dc in next 2 sc, work double decrease, dc in last sc: {8-9-11}{13-13-15} Shells.

Row 7: Ch 3, turn; work double decrease, dc in next 3 sc, ★ † skip next 2 sc, work Shell in next sc, skip next 2 sc †, dc in next sc; repeat from ★ across to last 12 sc, then repeat from † to † once, dc in next 3 sc, work double decrease, dc in last sc: {7-8-10}{12-12-14} Shells.

Row 9: Ch 3, turn; dc in next sc, ★ † skip next 2 sc, work Shell in next sc, skip next 2 sc †, dc in next sc; repeat from ★ across to last 7 sc, then repeat from † to † once, dc in last 2 sc: {8-9-11}{13-13-15} Shells.

Row 11: Ch 3, turn; work double decrease, dc in next sc, ★ skip next 2 sc, work Shell in next sc, skip next 2 sc, dc in next sc; repeat from ★ across to last 4 sc, work double decrease, dc in last sc: {7-8-10}{12-12-14} Shells.

Row 13: Ch 3, turn; work double decrease, dc in next 2 sc, ★ † skip next 2 sc, work Shell in next sc, skip next 2 sc †, dc in next sc; repeat from ★ across to last 11 sc, then repeat from † to † once, dc in next 2 sc, work double decrease, dc in last sc: {6-7-9}{11-11-13} Shells.

Row 15: Ch 3, turn; ★ skip next 2 sc, work Shell in next sc, skip next 2 sc, dc in next sc; repeat from ★ across: {7-8-10}{12-12-14} Shells.

Row 17: Ch 3, turn; dc decrease, dc in next sc, ★ skip next 2 sc, work Shell in next sc, skip next 2 sc, dc in next sc; repeat from ★ across to last 3 sc, dc decrease, dc in last sc: {6-7-9}{11-11-13} Shells.

Row 19: Ch 3, turn; work double decrease, dc in next 2 sc, ★ † skip next 2 sc, work Shell in next sc, skip next 2 sc †, dc in next sc; repeat from ★ across to last 11 sc, then repeat from † to † once, dc in next 2 sc, work double decrease, dc in last sc: {5-6-8}{10-10-12} Shells.

Row 21: Ch 3, turn; work double decrease, dc in next 3 sc, ★ † skip next 2 sc, work Shell in next sc, skip next 2 sc †, dc in next sc; repeat from ★ across to last 12 sc, then repeat from † to † once, dc in next 3 sc, work double decrease, dc in last sc: {4-5-7}{9-9-11} Shells.

Row 23: Ch 3, turn; dc in next sc, ★ † skip next 2 sc, work Shell in next sc, skip next 2 sc †, dc in next sc; repeat from ★ across to last 7 sc, then repeat from † to † once, dc in last 2 sc: {5-6-8}{10-10-12} Shells.

Row 25: Ch 3, turn; work double decrease, dc in next sc, ★ skip next 2 sc, work Shell in next sc, skip next 2 sc, dc in next sc; repeat from ★ across to last 4 sc, work double decrease, dc in last sc: {4-5-7}{9-9-11} Shells.

Row 26: Ch 1, turn; sc in each dc and in each ch-1 sp across: {29-35-47}{59-59-71} sc.

Sizes Extra Small & Small ONLY
Finish off.

Sizes Medium, Large, Extra Large, & 2X-Large ONLY
Row 27: Ch 3, turn; work double decrease, dc in next 2 sc, ★ † skip next 2 sc, work Shell in next sc, skip next 2 sc †, dc in next sc; repeat from ★ across to last 11 sc, then repeat from † to † once, dc in next 2 sc, work double decrease, dc in last sc: {6}{8-8-10} Shells.

Row 28: Ch 1, turn; sc in each dc and in each ch-1 sp across: {43}{55-55-67} sc.

Sizes Medium & Large ONLY
Finish off.

Sizes Extra Large & 2X-Large ONLY
Row 29: Ch 3, turn; ★ skip next 2 sc, work Shell in next sc, skip next 2 sc, dc in next sc; repeat from ★ across: {9-11} Shells.

Row 30: Ch 1, turn; sc in each dc and in each ch-1 sp across; finish off: {55-67} sc.

LEFT FRONT
Ch {53-59-65}{71-77-83}.

Row 1 (Right side)**:** Sc in second ch from hook and in each ch across: {52-58-64}{70-76-82} sc.

Note: Mark Row 1 as **right** side.

Row 2: Ch 1, turn; sc in each sc across.

Row 3: Ch 3, turn; dc in next 4 sc, ★ † skip next 2 sc, work Shell in next sc, skip next 2 sc †, dc in next sc; repeat from ★ across to last 11 sc, then repeat from † to † once, dc in last 6 sc: {7-8-9}{10-11-12} Shells.

Row 4 AND ALL EVEN-NUMBERED ROWS: Ch 1, turn; sc in each dc and in each ch-1 sp across.

Row 5: Ch 3, turn; dc in next sc, ★ skip next 2 sc, work Shell in next sc, skip next 2 sc, dc in next sc; repeat from ★ across to last 8 sc, skip next 2 sc, 3 dc in next sc, dc in last 5 sc: {7-8-9}{10-11-12} Shells.

Row 7: Ch 3, turn; dc decrease, dc in next 2 sc, ★ † skip next 2 sc, work Shell in next sc, skip next 2 sc †, dc in next sc; repeat from ★ across to last 11 sc, then repeat from † to † once, dc in last 6 sc: {7-8-9}{10-11-12} Shells.

Row 9: Ch 3, turn; ★ skip next 2 sc, work Shell in next sc, skip next 2 sc, dc in next sc; repeat from ★ across to last 8 sc, skip next 2 sc, 3 dc in next sc, dc in last 5 sc: {7-8-9}{10-11-12} Shells.

Row 11: Ch 3, turn; dc decrease, dc in next sc, ★ † skip next 2 sc, work Shell in next sc, skip next 2 sc †, dc in next sc; repeat from ★ across to last 11 sc, then repeat from † to † once, dc in last 6 sc: {7-8-9}{10-11-12} Shells.

Row 13: Ch 3, turn; dc decrease, dc in next 3 sc, ★ skip next 2 sc, work Shell in next sc, skip next 2 sc, dc in next sc; repeat from ★ across to last 8 sc, skip next 2 sc, 3 dc in next sc, dc in last 5 sc: {6-7-8}{9-10-11} Shells.

Instructions continued on page 114.

Row 15: Ch 3, turn; dc decrease, dc in next sc, 3 dc in next sc, skip next 2 sc, dc in next sc, ★ † skip next 2 sc, work Shell in next sc, skip next 2 sc †, dc in next sc; repeat from ★ across to last 11 sc, then repeat from † to † once, dc in last 6 sc: {6-7-8}{9-10-11} Shells.

Row 17: Ch 3, turn; dc decrease, dc in next sc, ★ skip next 2 sc, work Shell in next sc, skip next 2 sc, dc in next sc; repeat from ★ across to last 8 sc, skip next 2 sc, 3 dc in next sc, dc in last 5 sc: {6-7-8}{9-10-11} Shells.

Row 19: Ch 3, turn; skip next sc, work Shell in next sc, ★ skip next 2 sc, dc in next sc, skip next 2 sc, work Shell in next sc; repeat from ★ across to last 8 sc, skip next 2 sc, dc in last 6 sc: {7-8-9}{10-11-12} Shells.

Row 21: Ch 3, turn; dc in next 3 sc, ★ skip next 2 sc, work Shell in next sc, skip next 2 sc, dc in next sc; repeat from ★ across to last 8 sc, skip next 2 sc, 3 dc in next sc, dc in last 5 sc: {6-7-8}{9-10-11} Shells.

Row 23: Ch 3, turn; dc decrease, dc in next 4 sc, ★ † skip next 2 sc, work Shell in next sc, skip next 2 sc †, dc in next sc; repeat from ★ across to last 11 sc, then repeat from † to † once, dc in last 6 sc: {6-7-8}{9-10-11} Shells.

Row 25: Ch 3, turn; dc decrease, ★ skip next 2 sc, work Shell in next sc, skip next 2 sc, dc in next sc; repeat from ★ across to last 8 sc, skip next 2 sc, 3 dc in next sc, dc in last 5 sc: {6-7-8}{9-10-11} Shells.

Row 27: Ch 3, turn; dc decrease, dc in next 2 sc, ★ † skip next 2 sc, work Shell in next sc, skip next 2 sc †, dc in next sc; repeat from ★ across to last 11 sc, then repeat from † to † once, dc in last 6 sc: {6-7-8}{9-10-11} Shells.

Row 29: Ch 3, turn; ★ skip next 2 sc, work Shell in next sc, skip next 2 sc, dc in next sc; repeat from ★ across to last 8 sc, skip next 2 sc, 3 dc in next sc, dc in last 5 sc: {6-7-8}{9-10-11} Shells.

Row 31: Ch 3, turn; dc in next 3 sc, ★ † skip next 2 sc, work Shell in next sc, skip next 2 sc †, dc in next sc; repeat from ★ across to last 11 sc, then repeat from † to † once, dc in last 6 sc: {6-7-8}{9-10-11} Shells.

Row 33: Ch 3, turn; dc decrease, dc in next 4 sc, ★ skip next 2 sc, work Shell in next sc, skip next 2 sc, dc in next sc; repeat from ★ across to last 8 sc, skip next 2 sc, 3 dc in next sc, dc in last 5 sc: {5-6-7}{8-9-10} Shells.

Row 35: Ch 3, turn; dc in next 2 sc, ★ † skip next 2 sc, work Shell in next sc, skip next 2 sc †, dc in next sc; repeat from ★ across to last 11 sc, then repeat from † to † once, dc in last 6 sc: {6-7-8}{9-10-11} Shells.

Row 37: Ch 3, turn; dc decrease, dc in next 3 sc, ★ skip next 2 sc, work Shell in next sc, skip next 2 sc, dc in next sc; repeat from ★ across to last 8 sc, skip next 2 sc, 3 dc in next sc, dc in last 5 sc: {5-6-7}{8-9-10} Shells.

Row 39: Ch 3, turn; dc decrease, skip next sc, work Shell in next sc, ★ skip next 2 sc, dc in next sc, skip next 2 sc, work Shell in next sc; repeat from ★ across to last 8 sc, skip next 2 sc, dc in last 6 sc: {6-7-8}{9-10-11} Shells.

Row 41: Ch 3, turn; dc decrease, dc in next 2 sc, ★ skip next 2 sc, work Shell in next sc, skip next 2 sc, dc in next sc; repeat from ★ across to last 8 sc, skip next 2 sc, 3 dc in next sc, dc in last 5 sc: {5-6-7}{8-9-10} Shells.

Row 42: Ch 1, turn; sc in each dc and in each ch-1 sp across: {42-48-54}{60-66-72} sc.

RAGLAN ARMHOLE SHAPING

Row 1: Turn; slip st in first {6-6-6}{6-12-12} sc, ch 3, dc in next sc, ★ † skip next 2 sc, work Shell in next sc, skip next 2 sc †, dc in next sc; repeat from ★ across to last 11 sc, then repeat from † to † once, dc in last 6 sc: {5-6-7}{8-8-9} Shells.

Row 2 AND ALL EVEN-NUMBERED ROWS: Ch 1, turn; sc in each dc and in each ch-1 sp across.

Row 3: Ch 3, turn; work double decrease, dc in next sc, ★ skip next 2 sc, work Shell in next sc, skip next 2 sc, dc in next sc; repeat from ★ across to last 8 sc, skip next 2 sc, 3 dc in next sc, dc in last 5 sc: {4-5-6}{7-7-8} Shells.

Row 5: Ch 3, turn; work double decrease, dc in next 2 sc, ★ † skip next 2 sc, work Shell in next sc, skip next 2 sc †, dc in next sc; repeat from ★ across to last 11 sc, then repeat from † to † once, dc in last 6 sc: {4-5-6}{7-7-8} Shells.

Row 7: Ch 3, turn; work double decrease, dc in next 3 sc, ★ skip next 2 sc, work Shell in next sc, skip next 2 sc, dc in next sc; repeat from ★ across to last 8 sc, skip next 2 sc, 3 dc in next sc, dc in last 5 sc: {3-4-5}{6-6-7} Shells.

Row 9: Ch 3, turn; dc in next sc, ★ † skip next 2 sc, work Shell in next sc, skip next 2 sc †, dc in next sc; repeat from ★ across to last 11 sc, then repeat from † to † once, dc in last 6 sc: {4-5-6}{7-7-8} Shells.

Row 11: Ch 3, turn; work double decrease, dc in next sc, ★ skip next 2 sc, work Shell in next sc, skip next 2 sc, dc in next sc; repeat from ★ across to last 8 sc, skip next 2 sc, 3 dc in next sc, dc in last 5 sc: {3-4-5}{6-6-7} Shells.

Row 13: Ch 3, turn; work double decrease, dc in next 2 sc, ★ † skip next 2 sc, work Shell in next sc, skip next 2 sc †, dc in next sc; repeat from ★ across to last 11 sc, then repeat from † to † once, dc in last 6 sc: {3-4-5}{6-6-7} Shells.

Row 15: Ch 3, turn; ★ skip next 2 sc, work Shell in next sc, skip next 2 sc, dc in next sc; repeat from ★ across to last 8 sc, skip next 2 sc, 3 dc in next sc, dc in last 5 sc: {3-4-5}{6-6-7} Shells.

Row 17: Ch 3, turn; dc decrease, dc in next sc, ★ † skip next 2 sc, work Shell in next sc, skip next 2 sc †, dc in next sc; repeat from ★ across to last 8 sc, then repeat from † to † once, dc in last 3 sc: {3-4-5}{6-6-7} Shells.

Row 19: Ch 3, turn; work double decrease, dc in next 2 sc, ★ skip next 2 sc, work Shell in next sc, skip next 2 sc, dc in next sc; repeat from ★ across to last 8 sc, skip next 2 sc, 3 dc in next sc, dc in last 5 sc: {2-3-4}{5-5-6} Shells.

Row 20: Ch 1, turn; sc in each dc and in each ch-1 sp across.

Instructions continued on page 116.

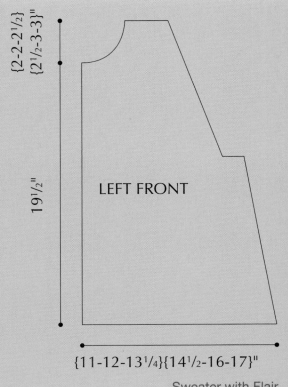

{2-2-2½}
{2½-3-3}"

19½"

LEFT FRONT

{11-12-13¼}{14½-16-17}"

NECK SHAPING

Row 1: Ch 3, turn; work double decrease, dc in next 3 sc, ★ skip next 2 sc, work Shell in next sc, skip next 2 sc, dc in next sc; repeat from ★ {0-1-2}{3-3-4} time(s) **more (see Zeros, page 125)**, leave remaining sc unworked: {1-2-3}{4-4-5} Shells.

Row 3: Ch 3, turn; dc in next sc, ★ skip next 2 sc, work Shell in next sc, skip next 2 sc, dc in next sc; repeat from ★ {0-1-2}{3-3-4} time(s) **more**, leave remaining sc unworked: {1-2-3}{4-4-5} Shells.

Size Extra Small ONLY
Row 5: Ch 3, turn; work double decrease, dc in next 4 sc: 6 dc.

Row 6: Ch 1, turn; sc in each dc across; finish off.

Size Small ONLY
Row 5: Ch 3, turn; work double decrease, dc in next sc, skip next 2 sc, work Shell in next sc, skip next 2 sc, dc in next sc, leave remaining sc unworked: one Shell.

Row 6: Ch 1, turn; sc in each dc and in ch-1 sp across; finish off: 9 sc.

Sizes Medium, Large, Extra Large, & 2X-Large ONLY
Row 5: Ch 3, turn; work double decrease, dc in next sc, ★ skip next 2 sc, work Shell in next sc, skip next 2 sc, dc in next sc; repeat from ★ {1}{2-2-3} times **more**, leave remaining sc unworked: {2}{3-3-4} Shells.

Row 7: Ch 3, turn; work double decrease, dc in next 2 sc, ★ skip next 2 sc, work Shell in next sc, skip next 2 sc, dc in next sc; repeat from ★ {0}{1-1-2} time(s) **more**, leave remaining sc unworked: {1}{2-2-3} Shells.

Row 8: Ch 1, turn; sc in each dc and in each ch-1 sp across: {10}{16-16-22} sc.

Sizes Medium & Large ONLY
Finish off.

Sizes Extra Large & 2X-Large ONLY
Row 9: Ch 3, turn; ★ skip next 2 sc, work Shell in next sc, skip next 2 sc, dc in next sc; repeat from ★ {1-2} time(s) **more**, leave remaining sc unworked: {2-3} Shells.

Row 10: Ch 1, turn; sc in each dc and in each ch-1 sp across; finish off: {13-19} dc.

RIGHT FRONT
Ch {53-59-65}{71-77-83}.

Row 1 (Right side)**:** Sc in second ch from hook and in each ch across: {52-58-64}{70-76-82} sc.

Note: Mark Row 1 as **right** side.

Row 2: Ch 1, turn; sc in each sc across.

Row 3: Ch 3, turn; dc in next 5 sc, ★ † skip next 2 sc, work Shell in next sc, skip next 2 sc †, dc in next sc; repeat from ★ across to last 11 sc, then repeat from † to † once, dc in last 5 sc: {7-8-9}{10-11-12} Shells.

Row 4 AND ALL EVEN-NUMBERED ROWS: Ch 1, turn; sc in each dc and in each ch-1 sp across.

Row 5: Ch 3, turn; dc in next 4 sc, 3 dc in next sc, ★ skip next 2 sc, dc in next sc, skip next 2 sc, work Shell in next sc; repeat from ★ across to last 4 sc, skip next 2 sc, dc in last 2 sc: {7-8-9}{10-11-12} Shells.

Row 7: Ch 3, turn; dc in next 5 sc, ★ † skip next 2 sc, work Shell in next sc, skip next 2 sc †, dc in next sc; repeat from ★ across to last 10 sc, then repeat from † to † once, dc in next 2 sc, dc decrease, dc in last sc: {7-8-9}{10-11-12} Shells.

Row 9: Ch 3, turn; dc in next 4 sc, 3 dc in next sc, ★ skip next 2 sc, dc in next sc, skip next 2 sc, work Shell in next sc; repeat from ★ across to last 3 sc, skip next 2 sc, dc in last sc: {7-8-9}{10-11-12} Shells.

Row 11: Ch 3, turn; dc in next 5 sc, ★ skip next 2 sc, work Shell in next sc, skip next 2 sc, dc in next sc; repeat from ★ across to last 3 sc, dc decrease, dc in last dc: {7-8-9}{10-11-12} Shells.

Row 13: Ch 3, turn; dc in next 4 sc, 3 dc in next sc, ★ skip next 2 sc, dc in next sc, skip next 2 sc, work Shell in next sc; repeat from ★ across to last 8 sc, skip next 2 sc, dc in next 3 sc, dc decrease, dc in last sc: {6-7-8}{9-10-11} Shells.

Row 15: Ch 3, turn; dc in next 5 sc, ★ skip next 2 sc, work Shell in next sc, skip next 2 sc, dc in next sc; repeat from ★ across to last 7 sc, skip next 2 sc, 3 dc in next sc, dc in next sc, dc decrease, dc in last sc: {6-7-8}{9-10-11} Shells.

Row 17: Ch 3, turn; dc in next 4 sc, 3 dc in next sc, ★ skip next 2 sc, dc in next sc, skip next 2 sc, work Shell in next sc; repeat from ★ across to last 6 sc, skip next 2 sc, dc in next sc, dc decrease, dc in last sc: {6-7-8}{9-10-11} Shells.

Row 19: Ch 3, turn; dc in next 5 sc, skip next 2 sc, work Shell in next sc, ★ skip next 2 sc, dc in next sc skip next 2 sc, work Shell in next sc; repeat from ★ across to last 2 sc, skip next sc, dc in next sc: {7-8-9}{10-11-12} Shells.

Row 21: Ch 3, turn; dc in next 3 sc, ch 1, skip next sc (buttonhole made), 3 dc in next sc, ★ skip next 2 sc, dc in next sc, skip next 2 sc, work Shell in next sc; repeat from ★ across to last 6 sc, skip next 2 sc, dc in last 4 sc: {6-7-8}{9-10-11} Shells.

Row 23: Ch 3, turn; dc in next 5 sc, ★ † skip next 2 sc, work Shell in next sc, skip next 2 sc †, dc in next sc; repeat from ★ across to last 7 sc, then repeat from † to † once, dc in next 4 sc, dc decrease, dc in last sc: {6-7-8}{9-10-11} Shells.

Row 25: Ch 3, turn; dc in next 4 sc, 3 dc in next sc, ★ skip next 2 sc, dc in next sc, skip next 2 sc, work Shell in next sc; repeat from ★ across to last 5 sc, skip next 2 sc, dc decrease, dc in last sc: {6-7-8}{9-10-11} Shells.

Row 27: Ch 3, turn; dc in next 5 sc, ★ † skip next 2 sc, work Shell in next sc, skip next 2 sc †, dc in next sc; repeat from ★ across to last 10 sc, then repeat from † to † once, dc in next 2 sc, dc decrease, dc in last sc: {6-7-8}{9-10-11} Shells.

Row 29: Ch 3, turn; dc in next 4 sc, 3 dc in next sc, ★ skip next 2 sc, dc in next sc, skip next 2 sc, work Shell in next sc; repeat from ★ across to last 3 sc, skip next 2 sc, dc in last sc: {6-7-8}{9-10-11} Shells.

Row 31: Ch 3, turn; dc in next 5 sc, ★ † skip next 2 sc, work Shell in next sc, skip next 2 sc †, dc in next sc; repeat from ★ across to last 9 sc, then repeat from † to † once, dc in last 4 sc: {6-7-8}{9-10-11} Shells.

Row 33: Ch 3, turn; dc in next 4 sc, 3 dc in next sc, ★ skip next 2 sc, dc in next sc, skip next 2 sc, work Shell in next sc; repeat from ★ across to last 9 sc, skip next 2 sc, dc in next 4 sc, dc decrease, dc in last sc: {5-6-7}{8-9-10} Shells.

Row 35: Ch 3, turn; dc in next 5 sc, ★ † skip next 2 sc, work Shell in next sc, skip next 2 sc †, dc in next sc; repeat from ★ across to last 8 sc, then repeat from † to † once, dc in last 3 sc: {6-7-8}{9-10-11} Shells.

Row 37: Ch 3, turn; dc in next 4 sc, 3 dc in next sc, ★ skip next 2 sc, dc in next sc, skip next 2 sc, work Shell in next sc; repeat from ★ across to last 8 sc, skip next 2 sc, dc in next 3 sc, dc decrease, dc in last sc: {5-6-7}{8-9-10} Shells.

Row 39: Ch 3, turn; dc in next 5 sc, ★ skip next 2 sc, work Shell in next sc, skip next 2 sc, dc in next sc; repeat from ★ across to last 7 sc, skip next 2 sc, work Shell in next sc, skip next sc, dc decrease, dc in last sc: {6-7-8}{9-10-11} Shells.

Row 41: Ch 3, turn; dc in next 3 sc, ch 1, skip next sc (buttonhole made), 3 dc in next sc, ★ skip next 2 sc, dc in next sc, skip next 2 sc, work Shell in next sc; repeat from ★ across to last 7 sc, skip next 2 sc, dc in next 2 sc, dc decrease, dc in last sc: {5-6-7}{8-9-10} Shells.

Row 42: Ch 1, turn; sc in each dc and in each ch-1 sp across: {42-48-54}{60-66-72} sc.

Instructions continued on page 118.

RAGLAN ARMHOLE SHAPING

Row 1: Ch 3, turn; dc in next 5 sc, ★ † skip next 2 sc, work Shell in next sc, skip next 2 sc †, dc in next sc; repeat from ★ {3-4-5}{6-6-7} times **more**, then repeat from † to † once, dc in next 2 sc, leave remaining sts unworked: {5-6-7}{8-8-9} Shells.

Row 2 AND ALL EVEN-NUMBERED ROWS: Ch 1, turn; sc in each dc dc and in each ch-1 sp across.

Row 3: Ch 3, turn; dc in next 4 sc, 3 dc in next sc, ★ skip next 2 sc, dc in next sc, skip next 2 sc, work Shell in next sc; repeat from ★ across to last 7 sc, skip next 2 sc, dc in next sc, work double decrease, dc in last sc: {4-5-6}{7-7-8} Shells.

Row 5: Ch 3, turn; dc in next 5 sc, ★ † skip next 2 sc, work Shell in next sc, skip next 2 sc †, dc in next sc; repeat from ★ across to last 11 sc, then repeat from † to † once, dc in next 2 sc, work double decrease, dc in last sc: {4-5-6}{7-7-8} Shells.

Row 7: Ch 3, turn; dc in next 4 sc, 3 dc in next sc, ★ skip next 2 sc, dc in next sc, skip next 2 sc, work Shell in next sc; repeat from ★ across to last 9 sc, skip next 2 sc, dc in next 3 sc, work double decrease, dc in last dc: {3-4-5}{6-6-7} Shells.

Row 9: Ch 3, turn; dc in next 5 sc, ★ † skip next 2 sc, work Shell in next sc, skip next 2 sc †, dc in next sc; repeat from ★ across to last 7 sc, then repeat from † to † once, dc in last 2 sc: {4-5-6}{7-7-8} Shells.

Row 11: Ch 3, turn; dc in next 4 sc, 3 dc in next sc, ★ skip next 2 sc, dc in next sc, skip next 2 sc, work Shell in next sc; repeat from ★ across to last 7 sc, skip next 2 sc, dc in next sc, work double decrease, dc in last sc: {3-4-5}{6-6-7} Shells.

Row 13: Ch 3, turn; dc in next 5 sc, ★ † skip next 2 sc, work Shell in next sc, skip next 2 sc †, dc in next sc; repeat from ★ across to last 11 sc, then repeat from † to † once, dc in next 2 sc, work double decrease, dc in last dc: {3-4-5}{6-6-7} Shells.

Row 15: Ch 3, turn; dc in next 4 sc, 3 dc in next sc, ★ skip next 2 sc, dc in next sc, skip next 2 sc, work Shell in next sc; repeat from ★ across to last 3 sc, skip next 2 sc, dc in last sc: {3-4-5}{6-6-7} Shells.

Row 17: Ch 3, turn; dc in next 3 dc, ch 1, skip next sc (buttonhole made), dc in next sc, ★ † skip next 2 sc, work Shell in next sc, skip next 2 sc †, dc in next sc; repeat from ★ across to last 9 sc, then repeat from † to † once, dc in next sc, dc decrease, dc in last sc: {3-4-5}{6-6-7} Shells.

Row 19: Ch 3, turn; dc in next 4 sc, 3 dc in next sc, ★ skip next 2 sc, dc in next sc, skip next 2 sc, work Shell in next sc; repeat from ★ across to last 8 sc, skip next 2 sc, dc in next 2 sc, work double decrease, dc in last sc: {2-3-4}{5-5-6} Shells.

Row 20: Ch 1, turn; sc in each dc and in each ch 1 sp across.

NECK SHAPING

Row 1: Turn; slip st in first 12 sc, ch 3, ★ skip next 2 sc, work Shell in next sc, skip next 2 sc, dc in next sc; repeat from ★ {0-1-2}{3-3-4} time(s) **more**, dc in next 2 sc, work double decrease, dc in last sc: {1-2-3}{4-4-5} Shells.

Row 3: Turn; slip st in first 4 sc, ch 3, ★ skip next 2 sc, work Shell in next sc, skip next 2 sc, dc in next sc; repeat from ★ {0-1-2}{3-3-4} time(s) **more**, dc in last sc: {1-2-3}{4-4-5} Shells.

Size Extra Small ONLY
Row 5: Ch 3, turn; dc in next 3 sc, work double decrease, dc in last sc: 6 dc.

Row 6: Ch 1, turn; sc in each dc across; finish off.

Size Small ONLY
Row 5: Turn; slip st in first 4 sc, ch 3, skip next 2 sc, work Shell in next sc, skip next 2 sc, dc in next sc, work double decrease, dc in last sc: one Shell.

Row 6: Ch 1, turn; sc in each dc and in each ch-1 sp across; finish off: 9 sc.

Sizes Medium, Large, Extra Large, & 2X-Large ONLY
Row 5: Turn; slip st in first 4 sc, ch 3, ★ skip next 2 sc, work Shell in next sc, skip next 2 sc, dc in next sc; repeat from ★ {1}{2-2-3} time(s) **more**, work double decrease, dc in last sc: {2}{3-3-4} Shells.

Row 7: Turn; slip st in first 4 sc, ch 3, ★ skip next 2 sc, work Shell in next sc, skip next 2 sc, dc in next sc; repeat from ★ {0}{1-1-2} time(s) **more**, dc in next sc, work double decrease, dc in last dc: {1}{2-2-3} Shells.

Row 8: Ch 1, turn; sc in each dc and in each ch-1 sp across: {10}{16-16-22} sc.

Medium & Large ONLY
Finish off.

Sizes Extra Large & 2X-Large ONLY
Row 9: Turn; slip st in first 4 sc, ch 3, ★ skip next 2 sc, work Shell in next sc, skip next 2 sc, dc in next sc; repeat from ★ across: {2-3} Shells.

Row 10: Ch 1, turn; sc in each dc and in each ch-1 sp across; finish off: {13-19} sc.

SLEEVE (Make 2)
Ch {94-94-100}{100-106-106}.

Row 1 (Right side): Sc in second ch from hook and in each ch across: {93-93-99}{99-105-105} sc.

Note: Mark Row 1 as **right** side.

Row 2: Ch 1, turn; sc in each sc across.

Row 3: Ch 3, turn; 3 dc in next sc, skip next 2 sc, dc in next sc, ★ skip next 2 sc, work Shell in next sc, skip next 2 sc, dc in next sc; repeat from ★ across to last 4 sc, skip next 2 sc, 3 dc in next sc, dc in last sc: {14-14-15}{15-16-16} Shells.

Row 4: Ch 1, turn; work beginning decrease, sc in each dc and in each ch-1 sp across to last 2 dc, sc decrease: {91-91-97}{97-103-103} sc.

Row 5: Ch 3, turn; ★ skip next 2 sc, work Shell in next sc, skip next 2 sc, dc in next sc; repeat from ★ across: {15-15-16}{16-17-17} Shells.

Row 6: Ch 1, turn; work beginning sc decrease, sc in each dc and in each ch-1 sp across to last 2 dc, sc decrease: {89-89-95}{95-101-101} sc.

Instructions continued on page 120.

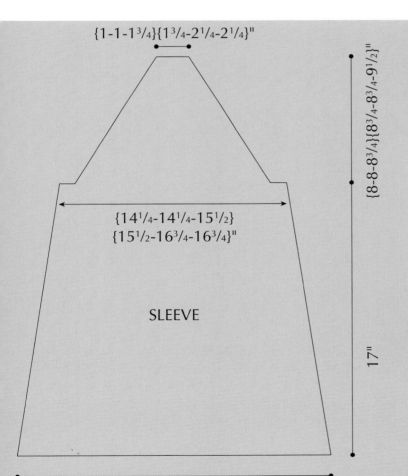

{1-1-1³/₄}{1³/₄-2¹/₄-2¹/₄}"

{8-8-8³/₄}{8³/₄-8³/₄-9¹/₂}"

{14¹/₄-14¹/₄-15¹/₂}
{15¹/₂-16³/₄-16³/₄}"

SLEEVE

17"

{19¹/₂-19¹/₂-20¹/₂}{20¹/₂-22-22}"

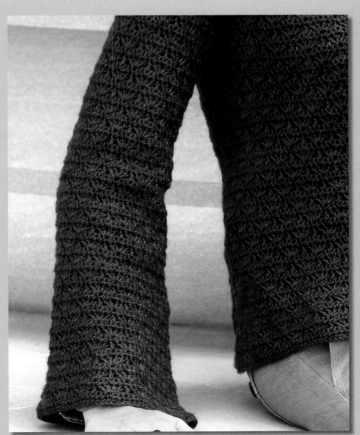

Row 7: Ch 3, turn; dc in next 2 sc, ★ † skip next 2 sc, work Shell in next sc, skip next 2 sc †, dc in next sc; repeat from ★ across to last 8 sc, then repeat from † to † once, dc in last 3 sc: {14-14-15}{15-16-16} Shells.

Row 8: Ch 1, turn; work beginning sc decrease, sc in each dc and in each ch-1 sp across to last 2 dc, sc decrease: {87-87-93}{93-99-99} sc.

Row 9: Ch 3, turn; 3 dc in next sc, skip next 2 sc, dc in next sc, ★ skip next 2 sc, work Shell in next sc, skip next 2 sc, dc in next sc; repeat from ★ across to last 4 sc, skip next 2 sc, 3 dc in next sc, dc in last sc: {13-13-14}{14-15-15} Shells.

Row 10: Ch 1, turn; work beginning sc decrease, sc in each dc and in each ch-1 sp across to last 2 dc, sc decrease: {85-85-91}{91-97-97} sc.

Row 11: Ch 3, turn; ★ skip next 2 sc, work Shell in next sc, skip next 2 sc, dc in next sc; repeat from ★ across: {14-14-15}{15-16-16} Shells.

Row 12: Ch 1, turn; work beginning sc decrease, sc in each dc and in each ch-1 sp across to last 2 dc, sc decrease: {83-83-89}{89-95-95} sc.

Row 13: Ch 3, turn; dc in next 2 sc, ★ † skip next 2 sc, work Shell in next sc, skip next 2 sc †, dc in next sc; repeat from ★ across to last 8 sc, then repeat from † to † once, dc in last 3 sc: {13-13-14}{14-15-15} Shells.

Row 14: Ch 1, turn; work beginning sc decrease, sc in each dc and in each ch-1 sp across to last 2 dc, sc decrease: {81-81-87}{87-93-93} sc.

Row 15: Ch 3, turn; 3 dc in next sc, skip next 2 sc, dc in next sc, ★ skip next 2 sc, work Shell in next sc, skip next 2 sc, dc in next sc; repeat from ★ across to last 4 sc, skip next 2 sc, 3 dc in next sc, dc in last sc: {12-12-13}{13-14-14} Shells.

Row 16: Ch 1, turn; sc in each dc and in each ch-1 sp across: {81-81-87}{87-93-93} sc.

Row 17: Ch 3, turn; dc in next sc, ★ † skip next 2 sc, work Shell in next sc, skip next 2 sc †, dc in next sc; repeat from ★ across to last 7 sc, then repeat from † to † once, dc in last 2 sc: {13-13-14}{14-15-15} Shells.

Row 18: Ch 1, turn; sc in each dc and in each ch-1 sp across: {81-81-87}{87-93-93} sc.

Row 19: Ch 3, turn; 3 dc in next sc, skip next 2 sc, dc in next sc, ★ skip next 2 sc, work Shell in next sc, skip next 2 sc, dc in next sc; repeat from ★ across to last 4 sc, skip next 2 sc, 3 dc in next sc, dc in last sc: {12-12-13}{13-14-14} Shells.

Row 20: Ch 1, turn; work beginning sc decrease, sc in each dc and in each ch-1 sp across to last 2 dc, sc decrease: {79-79-85}{85-91-91} sc.

Row 21: Ch 3, turn; ★ skip next 2 sc, work Shell in next sc, skip next 2 sc, dc in next sc; repeat from ★ across: {13-13-14}{14-15-15} Shells.

Row 22: Ch 1, turn; work beginning sc decrease, sc in each dc and in each ch-1 sp across to last 2 dc, sc decrease: {77-77-83}{83-89-89} sc.

Row 23: Ch 3, turn; dc in next 2 sc, ★ † skip next 2 sc, work Shell in next sc, skip next 2 sc †, dc in next sc; repeat from ★ across to last 8 sc, then repeat from † to † once, dc in last 3 sc: {12-12-13}{13-14-14} Shells.

Row 24: Ch 1, turn; work beginning sc decrease, sc in each dc and in each ch-1 sp across to last 2 dc, sc decrease: {75-75-81}{81-87-87} sc.

Row 25: Ch 3, turn; 3 dc in next sc, skip next 2 sc, dc in next sc, ★ skip next 2 sc, work Shell in next sc, skip next 2 sc, dc in next sc; repeat from ★ across to last 4 sc, skip next 2 sc, 3 dc in next sc, dc in last sc: {11-11-12}{12-13-13} Shells.

Row 26: Ch 1, turn; sc in each dc and in each ch-1 sp across: {75-75-81}{81-87-87} sc.

Row 27: Ch 3, turn; dc in next sc, ★ † skip next 2 sc, work Shell in next sc, skip next 2 sc †, dc in next sc; repeat from ★ across to last 7 sc, then repeat from † to † once, dc in last 2 sc: {12-12-13}{13-14-14} Shells.

Row 28: Ch 1, turn; work beginning sc decrease, sc in each dc and in each ch-1 sp across to last 2 dc, sc decrease: {73-73-79}{79-85-85} sc.

Row 29: Ch 3, turn; 2 dc in next sc, skip next sc, dc in next sc, ★ skip next 2 sc, work Shell in next sc, skip next 2 sc, dc in next sc; repeat from ★ across to last 3 sc, skip next sc, 2 dc in next sc, dc in last sc: {11-11-12}{12-13-13} Shells.

Row 30: Ch 1, turn; sc in each dc and in each ch-1 sp across.

Row 31: Ch 3, turn; ★ skip next 2 sc, work Shell in next sc, skip next 2 sc, dc in next sc; repeat from ★ across: {12-12-13}{13-14-14} Shells.

Row 32: Ch 1, turn; work beginning sc decrease, sc in each dc and in each ch-1 sp across to last 2 dc, sc decrease: {71-71-77}{77-83-83} sc.

Row 33: Ch 3, turn; dc in next 2 sc, ★ † skip next 2 sc, work Shell in next sc, skip next 2 sc †, dc in next sc; repeat from ★ across to last 8 sc, then repeat from † to † once, dc in last 3 sc: {11-11-12}{12-13-13} Shells.

Row 34: Ch 1, turn; sc in each dc and in each ch-1 sp across: {71-71-77}{77-83-83} sc.

Row 35: Ch 3, turn; dc in next sc, 3 dc in next sc, skip next 2 sc, dc in next sc, ★ skip next 2 sc, work Shell in next sc, skip next 2 sc, dc in next sc; repeat from ★ across to last 5 sc, skip next 2 sc, 3 dc in next sc, dc in last 2 sc: {10-10-11}{11-12-12} Shells.

Row 36: Ch 1, turn; sc in each dc and in each ch-1 sp across.

Row 37: Ch 3, turn; dc in next 2 sc, ★ † skip next 2 sc, work Shell in next sc, skip next 2 sc †, dc in next sc; repeat from ★ across to last 8 sc, then repeat from † to † once, dc in last 3 sc: {11-11-12}{12-13-13} Shells.

Row 38: Ch 1, turn; work beginning sc decrease, sc in each dc and in each ch-1 sp across to last 2 dc, sc decrease: {69-69-75}{75-81-81} sc.

Row 39: Ch 3, turn; 3 dc in next sc, skip next 2 sc, dc in next sc, ★ skip next 2 sc, work Shell in next sc, skip next 2 sc, dc in next sc; repeat from ★ across to last 4 sc, skip next 2 sc, 3 dc in next sc, dc in last sc: {10-10-11}{11-12-12} Shells.

Row 40: Ch 1, turn; sc in each dc and in each ch-1 sp across.

Row 41: Ch 3, turn; dc in next sc, ★ † skip next 2 sc, work Shell in next sc, skip next 2 sc †, dc in next sc; repeat from ★ across to last 7 sc, then repeat from † to † once, dc in last 2 sc: {11-11-12}{12-13-13} Shells.

Row 42: Ch 1, turn; sc in each dc and in each ch-1 sp across.

Rows 43-54: Repeat Rows 39-42, 3 times.

CAP SHAPING
Row 1: Turn; slip st in first {5-5-5}{5-11-11} sc, ch 3, ★ skip next 2 sc, work Shell in next sc, skip next 2 sc, dc in next sc; repeat from ★ {9-9-10}{10-9-9} times **more**, leave remaining sts unworked: {10-10-11}{11-10-10} Shells.

Row 2: Ch 1, turn; work beginning sc decrease, sc in each dc and in each ch-1 sp across to last 2 dc, sc decrease: {59-59-65}{65-59-59} sc.

Row 3: Ch 3, turn; dc in next 2 sc, ★ † skip next 2 sc, work Shell in next sc, skip next 2 sc †, dc in next sc; repeat from ★ across to last 8 sc, then repeat from † to † once, dc in last 3 sc: {9-9-10}{10-9-9} Shells.

Row 4: Ch 1, turn; work beginning sc decrease, sc decrease, sc in each dc and in each ch-1 sp across to last 4 dc, sc decrease twice: {55-55-61}{61-55-55} sc.

Row 5: Ch 3, turn; 2 dc in next sc, skip next sc, dc in next sc, ★ skip next 2 sc, work Shell in next sc, skip next 2 sc, dc in next sc; repeat from ★ across to last 3 sc, skip next sc, 2 dc in next sc, dc in last sc: {8-8-9}{9-8-8} Shells.

Instructions continued on page 122.

Row 6: Ch 1, turn; work beginning sc decrease, sc decrease, sc in each dc and in each ch-1 sp across to last 4 dc, sc decrease twice: {51-51-57}{57-51-51} sc.

Row 7: Ch 3, turn; 3 dc in next sc, skip next 2 sc, dc in next sc, ★ skip next 2 sc, work Shell in next sc, skip next 2 sc, dc in next sc; repeat from ★ across to last 4 sc, skip next 2 sc, 3 dc in next sc, dc in last sc: {7-7-8}{8-7-7} Shells.

Row 8: Ch 1, turn; work beginning sc decrease, sc in each dc and in each ch-1 sp across to last 2 dc, sc decrease: {49-49-55}{55-49-49} sc.

Row 9: Ch 3, turn; ★ skip next 2 sc, work Shell in next sc, skip next 2 sc, dc in next sc; repeat from ★ across: {8-8-9}{9-8-8} Shells.

Row 10: Ch 1, turn; work beginning sc decrease, sc decrease, sc in each dc and in each ch-1 sp across to last 4 sts, sc decrease twice: {45-45-51}{51-45-45} sc.

Row 11: Ch 3, turn; dc in next sc, ★ † skip next 2 sc, work Shell in next sc, skip next 2 sc †, dc in next sc; repeat from ★ across to last 7 sc, then repeat from † to † once, dc in last 2 sc: {7-7-8}{8-7-7} Shells.

Row 12: Ch 1, turn; work beginning sc decrease, sc decrease, sc in each dc and in each ch-1 sp across to last 4 dc, sc decrease twice: {41-41-47}{47-41-41} sc.

Row 13: Ch 3, turn; dc decrease, ★ † skip next 2 sc, work Shell in next sc, skip next 2 sc †, dc in next sc; repeat from ★ across to last 8 sc, then repeat from † to † once, dc decrease, dc in last sc: {6-6-7}{7-6-6} Shells.

Row 14: Ch 1, turn; work beginning sc decrease, sc decrease, sc in each dc and in each ch-1 sp across to last 4 dc, sc decrease twice: {35-35-41}{41-35-35} sc.

Row 15: Ch 3, turn; dc decrease, ★ † skip next 2 sc, work Shell in next sc, skip next 2 sc †, dc in next sc; repeat from ★ across to last 8 sc, then repeat from † to † once, dc decrease, dc in last sc: {5-5-6}{6-5-5} Shells.

Row 16: Ch 1, turn; work beginning sc decrease, sc decrease, sc in each dc and in each ch-1 sp across to last 4 dc, sc decrease twice: {29-29-35}{35-29-29} sc.

Row 17: Ch 3, turn; dc decrease, ★ † skip next 2 sc, work Shell in next sc, skip next 2 sc †, dc in next sc; repeat from ★ across to last 8 sc, then repeat from † to † once, dc decrease, dc in last sc: {4-4-5}{5-4-4} Shells.

Row 18: Ch 1, turn; work beginning sc decrease, sc decrease, sc in each dc and in each ch-1 sp across to last 4 dc, sc decrease twice: {23-23-29}{29-23-23} sc.

Row 19: Ch 3, turn; dc decrease, ★ † skip next 2 sc, work Shell in next sc, skip next 2 sc †, dc in next sc; repeat from ★ across to last 8 sc, then repeat from † to † once, dc decrease, dc in last sc: {3-3-4}{4-3-3} Shells.

Sizes Extra Small, Small, Medium, & Large ONLY
Row 20: Ch 1, turn; work beginning sc decrease, sc decrease, sc in each dc and in each ch-1 sp across to last 4 dc, sc decrease twice: {17-17-23}{23} sc.

Row 21: Ch 3, turn; dc decrease, ★ † skip next 2 sc, work Shell in next sc, skip next 2 sc †, dc in next sc; repeat from ★ across to last 8 sc, then repeat from † to † once, dc decrease, dc in last sc: {2-2-3}{3} Shells.

Sizes Extra Small & Small ONLY
Row 22: Ch 1, turn; work beginning sc decrease, sc decrease, sc in each dc and in each ch-1 sp across to last 4 dc, sc decrease twice: 11 sc.

Row 23: Ch 3, turn; dc decrease, skip next 2 sc, work Shell in next sc, skip next 2 sc, dc decrease, dc in last sc: one Shell.

Row 24: Ch 1, turn; work beginning sc decrease, sc decrease, sc in next ch-1 sp, sc decrease twice: 5 sc.

Row 25: Ch 3, turn; dc in next 4 sc.

Row 26: Ch 1, turn; sc in each dc across; finish off.

Sizes Medium and Large ONLY
Row 22: Ch 1, turn; work beginning sc decrease, sc in each dc and in each ch-1 sp across to last 2 dc, sc decrease: 19 sc.

Row 23: Ch 3, turn; dc decrease, ★ dc in next sc, skip next 2 sc, work Shell in next sc, skip next 2 sc; repeat from ★ once **more**, dc in next sc, dc decrease, dc in last sc: 2 Shells.

Row 24: Ch 1, turn; work beginning sc decrease, sc in each dc and in each ch-1 sp across to last 2 dc, sc decrease: 15 sc.

Row 25: Ch 3, turn; dc decrease, dc in next 2 sc, skip next 2 sc, work Shell in next sc, skip next 2 sc, dc in next 2 sc, dc decrease, dc in last sc: one Shell.

Row 26: Ch 1, turn; work beginning sc decrease, sc in each dc and in each ch-1 sp across to last 2 dc, sc decrease: 11 sc.

Row 27: Ch 3, turn; dc decrease, dc in next 5 sc, dc decrease, dc in last sc: 9 dc.

Row 28: Ch 1, turn; sc in each dc across; finish off.

Sizes Extra Large & 2X-Large ONLY
Row 20: Ch 1, turn; work beginning sc decrease, sc in each dc and in each ch-1 sp across to last 2 dc, sc decrease: 19 sc.

Row 21: Ch 3, turn; dc in next 3 sc, † skip next 2 sc, work Shell in next sc, skip next 2 sc †, dc in next sc; repeat from † to † once, dc in last 4 sc: 2 Shells.

Row 22: Ch 1, turn; work beginning sc decrease, sc in each dc and in each ch-1 sp across to last 2 dc, sc decrease: 17 sc.

Row 23: Ch 3, turn; dc in next sc, 3 dc in next sc, skip next 2 sc, dc in next sc, skip next 2 sc, work Shell in next sc, skip next 2 sc, dc in next sc, skip next 2 sc, 3 dc in next sc, dc in last 2 sc: one Shell.

Row 24: Ch 1, turn; work beginning sc decrease, sc in each dc and in ch-1 sp across to last 2 dc, sc decrease: 15 sc.

Row 25: Ch 3, turn; ★ dc in next sc, skip next 2 sc, work Shell in next sc, skip next 2 sc; repeat from ★ once **more**, dc in last 2 sc: 2 Shells.

Row 26: Ch 1, turn; work beginning sc decrease, sc in each dc and in each ch-1 sp across to last 2 dc, sc decrease: 13 sc.

Row 27: Ch 3, turn; dc in next 3 sc, skip next 2 sc, work Shell in next sc, skip next 2 sc, dc in last 4 sc: one Shell.

Row 28: Ch 1, turn; work beginning sc decrease, sc in each dc and in ch-1 sp across to last 2 dc, sc decrease: 11 sc.

Row 29: Ch 3, turn; dc in next sc and in each sc across.

Row 30: Ch 1, turn; sc in each dc across; finish off.

FINISHING
Weave Sleeves to Sweater *(Fig. 6, page 127)*.

Weave underarm and side in one continuous seam.

NECK EDGING
Row 1: With **right** side facing, join yarn with sc in first sc on Right Front; sc evenly across to Left Corner neck edge.

Rows 2 and 3: Ch 1, turn; sc in each sc across decreasing 3 sts across neck Shaping of each front.

Finish off.

Sew buttons to Left Front opposite buttonholes.

General Instructions

ABBREVIATIONS

BPdc	Back Post double crochet(s)
BPtr	Back Post treble crochet(s)
CC	Contrasting Color
ch(s)	chain(s)
cm	centimeters
dc	double crochet(s)
FPdc	Front Post double crochet(s)
FPtr	Front Post treble crochet(s)
hdc	half double crochet(s)
MC	Main Color
mm	millimeters
Rnd(s)	Round(s)
sc	single crochet(s)
sp(s)	space(s)
st(s)	stitch(es)
YO	yarn over

★ — work instructions following ★ as many **more** times as indicated in addition to the first time.

† to † — work all instructions from first † to second † **as many** times as specified.

( ) or [ ] — work enclosed instructions **as many** times as specified by the number immediately following **or** work all enclosed instructions in the stitch or space indicated **or** contains explanatory remarks.

colon (:) — the number(s) given after a colon at the end of a row or round denote(s) the number of stitches you should have on that row or round.

GAUGE

Exact gauge is **essential** for proper fit.

Before beginning your project, make the sample swatch given in the individual instructions in the yarn and hook specified.

After completing the swatch, measure it, counting your stitches and rows carefully. If your swatch is larger or smaller than specified, **make another, changing hook size to get the correct gauge**. Keep trying until you find the size hook that will give you the specified gauge. Once proper gauge is obtained, measure width of garment approximately every 3" (7.5 cm) to be sure gauge remains consistent.

HINTS

As in all garments, good finishing techniques make a big difference in the quality of the piece. Make a habit of taking care of loose ends as you work. Thread a yarn needle with the yarn end. With **wrong** side facing, weave the needle through several stitches, then reverse the direction and weave it back through several stitches. When the ends are secure, clip them off close to the work.

CROCHET TERMINOLOGY		
UNITED STATES		INTERNATIONAL
slip stitch (slip st)	=	single crochet (sc)
single crochet (sc)	=	double crochet (dc)
half double crochet (hdc)	=	half treble crochet (htr)
double crochet (dc)	=	treble crochet(tr)
treble crochet (tr)	=	double treble crochet (dtr)
double treble crochet (dtr)	=	triple treble crochet (ttr)
triple treble crochet (tr tr)	=	quadruple treble crochet (qtr)
skip	=	miss

■□□□ **BEGINNER**		Projects for first-time crocheters using basic stitches. Minimal shaping.
■■□□ **EASY**		Projects using yarn with basic stitches, repetitive stitch patterns, simple color changes, and simple shaping and finishing.
■■■□ **INTERMEDIATE**		Projects using a variety of techniques, such as basic lace patterns or color patterns, mid-level shaping and finishing.
■■■■ **EXPERIENCED**		Projects with intricate stitch patterns, techniques and dimension, such as non-repeating patterns, multi-color techniques, fine threads, small hooks, detailed shaping and refined finishing.

MARKERS

Markers are used to help distinguish the beginning of a pattern or to mark the beginning of a round. Place a 2" (5 cm) scrap piece of yarn before the first stitch of each round, moving the marker after each round is complete.

JOINING WITH SC

When instructed to join with sc, begin with a slip knot on hook. Insert hook in stitch or space indicated, YO and pull up a loop, YO and draw through both loops on hook.

JOINING WITH DC

When instructed to join with dc, begin with a slip knot on hook. YO, holding loop on hook, insert hook in stitch or space indicated, YO and pull up a loop (3 loops on hook), (YO and draw through 2 loops on hook) twice.

ZEROS

To consolidate the length of an involved pattern, Zeros are sometimes used so that all sizes can be combined. For example, increase every sixth row 5{1-0} time(s) means the first size would increase 5 times, the second size would increase once, and the largest size would do nothing.

BACK OR FRONT LOOP ONLY

Work only in loop(s) indicated by arrow *(Fig. 1)*.

Fig. 1

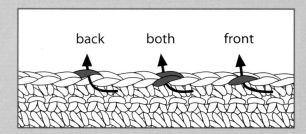

Yarn Weight Symbol & Names	LACE 0	SUPER FINE 1	FINE 2	LIGHT 3	MEDIUM 4	BULKY 5	SUPER BULKY 6
Type of Yarns in Category	Fingering, 10-count crochet thread	Sock, Fingering Baby	Sport, Baby	DK, Light Worsted	Worsted, Afghan, Aran	Chunky, Craft, Rug	Bulky, Roving
Crochet Gauge* Ranges in Single Crochet to 4" (10 cm)	32-42 double crochets**	21-32 sts	16-20 sts	12-17 sts	11-14 sts	8-11 sts	5-9 sts
Advised Hook Size Range	Steel*** 6,7,8 Regular hook B-1	B-1 to E-4	E-4 to 7	7 to I-9	I-9 to K-10.5	K-10.5 to M-13	M-13 and larger

*GUIDELINES ONLY: The chart above reflects the most commonly used gauges and hook sizes for specific yarn categories.

** Lace weight yarns are usually crocheted on larger-size hooks to create lacy openwork patterns. Accordingly, a gauge range is difficult to determine. Always follow the gauge stated in your pattern.

*** Steel crochet hooks are sized differently from regular hooks—the higher the number the smaller the hook, which is the reverse of regular hook sizing.

CROCHET HOOKS	
Metric mm	**U.S.**
2.25	B-1
2.75	C-2
3.25	D-3
3.5	E-4
3.75	F-5
4	G-6
5	H-8
5.5	I-9
6	J-10
6.5	K-10½
9	N
10	P
15	Q

FREE LOOPS OF A CHAIN

When instructed to work in free loops of a chain, work in loop indicated by arrow (*Fig. 2*).

Fig. 2

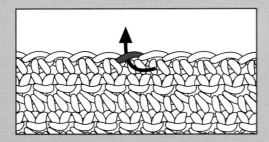

CHANGING COLORS

Work the last stitch to within one step of completion, drop yarn, hook new yarn (*Fig. 3*) and draw through all loops on hook. Do **not** cut old yarn.

Fig. 3

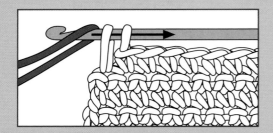

POST STITCH

Work around post of stitch indicated, inserting hook in direction of arrow (*Fig. 4*).

Fig. 4

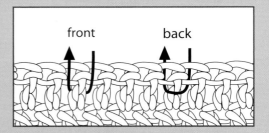

INCREASING EVENLY ACROSS A ROW

Add one to the number of increases required and divide that number into the number of stitches. Subtract one from the result and the new number is the approximate number of stitches to be worked between each increase. Adjust the number as needed.

WORKING IN SPACE BEFORE A STITCH

When instructed to work in space **before** a stitch or in spaces **between** stitches, insert hook in space indicated by arrow (*Fig. 5*).

Fig. 5

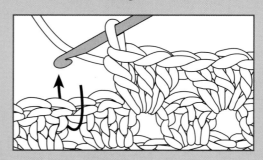

WEAVING SEAMS

With the **right** side of both pieces facing you and edges even, sew through both sides once to secure the beginning of the seam, leaving an ample yarn end to weave in later. Insert the needle from **right** to **left** through one strand on each piece *(Fig. 6)*. Bring the needle around and insert it from **right** to **left** through the next strand on both pieces. Continue in this manner, drawing seam together as you work.

Fig. 6

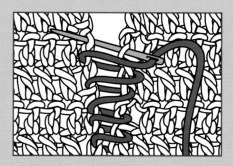

WHIPSTITCH

With **wrong** sides together, sew through both pieces once to secure the beginning of the seam, leaving an ample yarn end to weave in later. Insert the needle from **back** to **front** through two strands on each piece *(Fig. 7)*. Bring the needle around and insert it from **back** to **front** through the next strands on both pieces.
Repeat along the edge, being careful to match stitches.

Fig. 7

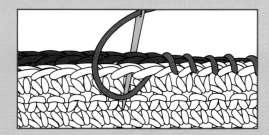

REVERSE SINGLE CROCHET
(abbreviated reverse sc)

Working from **left** to **right**, ★ insert hook in st to right of hook *(Fig. 8a)*, YO and draw through, under and to left of loop on hook (2 loops on hook) *(Fig. 8b)*, YO and draw through both loops on hook *(Fig. 8c) (reverse sc made, Fig. 8d)*; repeat from ★ around.

Fig. 8a

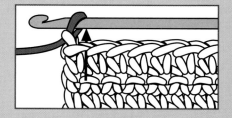

Fig. 8b

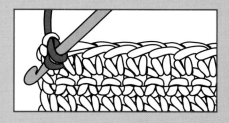

Fig. 8c

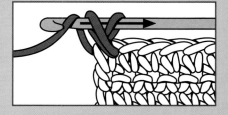

Fig. 8d

Yarn Information

The items in this book were made using a variety of yarns. Any brand of the specified weight of yarn may be used. It is best to refer to the yardage/meters when determining how many balls, skeins, or hanks to purchase. Remember, to achieve the same look, it is the weight of yarn that is important, not the brand of yarn.

For your convenience, listed below are the specific yarns used to create our photography models.

CAREFREE CARDIGAN
Naturally Caron® Country
#0018 Spice House

BUTTONS & SHELLS JACKET
Naturally Caron® Spa
#0008 Misty Taupe

PUFF-SLEEVED CARDIGAN
Tahki Yarns Savoy
#004 Light Olive

DOUBLE-UP JACKET
Caron® Simply Soft® Shadows
#0005 Soft Merino

ALL-BUTTONED-UP VEST
Lion Brand® Microspun
#144 Lilac

CLASSICAL JACKET
Cascade Yarns Eco Alpaca
#1518 Grey

BLUE HEAVEN SWEATER
Naturally Caron® Country
#0021 Peacock

SOMETHING SPECIAL CARDIGAN
Naturally Caron® Spa
#0007 Naturally

OPENWORK JACKET
Moda Dea™ Tweedle Dee™
#8913 Grape Jam

BEST BOUCLÉ CARDIGAN
Crystal Palace Bamboozle
Variegated - #9809 Fall Herbs
Red - #0502 Burgundy

BELTED PANT COAT
Bernat® Denimstyle
#03044 Sweatshirt

WEEKEND WARMER SWEATER
Lion Brand® Lion® Cashmere Blend
#124 Camel

NICE STRIPES VEST
Naturally Caron® Spa
MC (Blue) - #0005 Ocean Spray
CC (Green) - #0004 Green Sheen

ELEGANT SWING COAT
Cascade Yarn Eco Alpaca
#1510 Natural

SWEATER WITH FLAIR
Lion Brand® Microspun
#126 Coffee